FOLLOWING CHRIST

FOLLOWING CHRIST

Faith and Life Series

BOOK SIX

Ignatius Press, San Francisco
Catholics United for the Faith, New Rochelle

Nihil Obstat: Rev. Msgr. Daniel V. Flynn, J.C.D.
                Censor Librorum
Imprimatur: + Joseph T. O'Keefe
                Vicar General, New York

   Director: Rev. Msgr. Eugene Kevane, Ph.D.
   Assistant Director and General Editor: Patricia I. Puccetti, M.A.
   Writer: Joseph C. DiCarlo, Jr., M.A.

Catholics United for the Faith, Inc., and Ignatius Press gratefully acknowledge the guidance and
assistance of Reverend Monsignor Eugene Kevane, Director of the Pontifical Catechetical Institute,
Diocese of Arlington, Virginia, in the production of this series. The series intends to implement the
authentic approach in Catholic catechesis given to the Church in the recent documents of the Holy
See and in particular the Conference of Joseph Cardinal Ratzinger on ''Sources and Transmission
of Faith''.

CONTENTS

INTRODUCTION

Jesus has promised that he will be with us to the end of the world. He is with each of us, personally, in every step of our life. What is the special ingredient that Jesus adds to life that changes it from a dull chore to a rich adventure? The special ingredient is *love*. Jesus tells us that he came so that we "may have life and have it more abundantly". (Jn 10:10)

But perhaps we have heard that word *love* and it sounds magical, unreal. Well, this year we will be getting very practical. Before you build a house you need a blueprint. Even God, before he made the first man, had a plan for his body and soul—he planned every bone and every muscle, every nerve, every organ, every blood cell. We have a plan to lay the foundation of our lives: God's law.

Law is necessary if we are to have order in life, and without order there can be no happiness. All life is based on law. God planned the entire universe with very precise laws to guide every part of it, both very little things and very great. But everything we see around us—except human beings—obeys without choice. Men are not machines. We have free

will. We have the dignity of choice. We are invited to obey God's laws. And it is especially now, at this point in your lives, that the choice is offered to you in a new way. Life in Jesus is not for those who are lazy, indifferent, and selfish. But what would this invitation be without Jesus? Men have never lived together without laws. But no one has ever offered a better reason to live by law than Jesus—and that reason is love. There can be no real love without law; without law, love becomes mere sentimentality. But without love, law can become a fearful burden.

When he was asked which was the greatest commandment of God's law, Jesus said that love of God and neighbor sum up all the laws. We live by God's law, therefore, because we love God and each other. That makes all the difference.

What is being held out to you here is the invitation to become closely united with Jesus. The rewards are great. Jesus is always challenging us, always expecting more from us—and always giving us the graces we need to meet his demands.

PART ONE

The Ten Commandments

CHAPTER 1

God Gives Us the Law

If we observe the world around us we will see that there is a certain order or consistency in the way things happen. When we throw a stone in the air it falls back to the ground. We say it does that because of the law of gravity. Wild geese will fly for miles and miles to return every year to the same place to nest and hatch their goslings. It is said that they do that by instinct. And if we look at men now and through the ages, in different countries and cultures, we find that they always have a rule about right and wrong: "Do good and avoid evil." Human beings all over the earth have the idea that they ought to behave in a certain way.

Now, the difference between this rule of human behavior and the law of gravity or instinct is that the law of gravity or instinct tells us what things *do*, and the rule of human behavior tells us what we *ought* to do. In other words, the stone or goose has no choice in the matter. The stone doesn't decide to fall back to earth—it must. But while the rule of human behavior may tell us what is right and wrong to do, we are still free to decide just what we will do.

This presents a problem or two. The first is that though all men might agree that we should "do good and avoid evil", they don't always agree about what is good and what is evil in our acts. In fact, people are often mistaken as to what behavior is right and wrong. So how can we know for sure?

The second problem concerns our motivation to follow this law of human behavior. Since, unlike the stone obeying gravity, men aren't forced to act in accord with law but may freely choose, why do they?

The Master Plan

So where can we find the solution to these problems? Well, as you probably know, the best way is to look to the Master Planner and see what he had in mind.

As we all know, God is the Creator and Lord of Heaven and earth. In his great wisdom he made the universe and governs it all. Now, just as he made the law of gravity and instinct, he made all men with this notion of doing good and avoiding evil. But he also made men with free will, allowing them to decide for themselves what they would do.

Well, we all remember what happened when Adam made his choice. One of the results of original sin is that it is harder for all men to know what is right and wrong and to behave accordingly. And if we read the beginning of the Old Testament we can easily see that men soon made a mess of things acting on their own.

But God promised Adam that he would not abandon us and would give us a means of salvation. So God called upon Abraham and made him the father of his chosen people. And when God wanted to establish his cove-

nant with the Israelites, to show that he would be their God and they would be his people, he gave them the Decalogue—the Ten Commandments. God wanted his people to know what was right and wrong and what was pleasing to him, for he was preparing them for a special role in salvation history.

Some people think that God simply wanted obedience to a set of rules. But what he really wants is a particular kind of people. He gave his people a law to teach and guide them in every part of their lives.

Fulfillment of the Law

When Jesus came to establish the New Covenant, he did not set aside the Old Law, the Ten Commandments, but completed them. He said: "Do not think that I have come to abolish the law and the prophets. I have come, not to abolish them, but to fulfill them." (Mt 5:17) Jesus teaches that the foundation of all law is love: to love God above all things, with one's whole mind and heart and soul, and to love one's neighbor as oneself. Jesus wants all men to turn their minds and hearts to God with love. Disobeying any of the Ten Commandments is a failure to love either God or our neighbor.

Conscience

But how do we know that one action is right and another wrong? Along with free will God has given each man the ability to judge if

12

something is right or wrong. This ability is called *conscience*. Our conscience is a very practical tool. It tells us what would be right or wrong behavior in a given situation. We are to obey our conscience, for God gave it to us so that we could live according to his law.

Now, every person is born with a conscience, and even a member of some primitive tribe that has never come into contact with civilization has the same law in his heart to do good and avoid evil. And his tribe will probably have some code of what they think is right and wrong. Before God he will be responsible for doing what he thinks is right and not doing what he thinks is wrong. In this way he can please God. But his code of behavior might differ somewhat from the Ten Commandments. Since he has had no contact with the Commandments, he will not be held responsible for obeying them. But his conscience is faulty.

A conscience has to be taught—and taught correctly. We call this "forming" a conscience. The conscience of the primitive man, since it was not formed correctly, is called an incorrect conscience. Since he could do nothing about that, he will not be held responsible for his incorrect conscience. But all men who have access to the Word of God have a responsibility to form a correct conscience.

God has given us the means to form our consciences correctly. He has revealed truths about himself and given us the Ten Commandments. To live according to the will of God we must follow and obey them, and if we disregard or break God's law we sin.

But besides giving us the law he has given us reasons why we should want to follow it. First, God is the giver and author of that law, and since he is our Creator he knows what is best for us. The observance of the law is necessary for our salvation.

But even more compelling is the knowledge of the great love God has for us. Jesus tells us: "If you love me you will keep my commandments." (Jn 14:21) What better way do we have of showing our love for God than by doing what he asks of us?

Words to Know:

Covenant   Ten Commandments
    Decalogue   conscience

The Ten Commandments

1. I am the Lord your God; you shall not have strange gods before me.
2. You shall not take the Name of the Lord your God in vain.
3. Remember to keep holy the Lord's Day.
4. Honor your father and mother.
5. You shall not kill.
6. You shall not commit adultery.
7. You shall not steal.
8. You shall not bear false witness against your neighbor.
9. You shall not covet your neighbor's wife.
10. You shall not covet your neighbor's goods.

"Do not think that I have come to abolish the law and the prophets. I have come, not to abolish them, but to fulfill them." (Matthew 5:17)

Q. 1 *What must we do to live according to the will of God?*

To live according to the will of God we must believe the truths which he has revealed and obey his commandments, with the help of his grace, which we obtain by means of the sacraments and prayer.

Q. 2 *What are the commandments of God?*

The commandments of God, called the Decalogue, are the moral laws which God gave to Moses on Mount Sinai in the Old Testament, and which Jesus Christ perfected in the New Testament.

Q. 3 *What is the foundation of all our duties toward God and neighbor?*

The foundation of all our duties toward God and neighbor is charity, as Jesus Christ explained: the greatest and first commandment is the love of God, and the second is love of neighbor; upon these two commandments depends the whole law and the prophets.

Q. 4 *Are we obliged to keep the commandments of God?*

Yes, we are obliged to keep the commandments of God, because they are imposed on us by him who is our supreme Ruler, and they can be known by sound reason.

Q. 5 *Does he who breaks the commandments of God sin gravely?*

He who deliberately breaks even one commandment of God in a serious matter sins gravely against God, and thus merits hell.

CHAPTER 2

The First Commandment In Our Own Day

The First Commandment of God is:

"I am the Lord your God; you shall not have strange gods before me."

This commandment requires all men to recognize or acknowledge God as the one true God, Creator and Lord of all things, and to worship and adore him as our God. This is demanded of us because as creatures we owe everything to God; we are completely dependent on him. By our reverence and worship we acknowledge our debt and gratitude to our Creator.

To give God loving worship we must believe in him and believe all that he has revealed to us. This means that we must learn more about God, especially if he has given us the means to do this; we have no excuse for being ignorant about God and his truths.

Just as this commandment requires certain behavior from us, it also forbids us to act in any way contrary to what we owe God. It is wrong if we are superstitious or impious, which means being irreverent and disrespectful of God or sacred things. It is also wrong if we willfully doubt some truth about God or refuse to know what we should about God and our religion. There are times when some

people are so willful that they publicly acknowledge their disbelief in or disagreement with the truths of the faith. This is called heresy—the denying or disagreeing with one particular truth, or apostasy—deserting or leaving the true religion.

Strange Gods

We have read about people in ancient times who used to worship idols—false gods, things like golden calves. Remember when the Israelites worshipped the golden calf in the desert before God gave them the law? This is called idolatry. We don't run into too many people who worship golden calves, but many still place "strange gods" before God in their lives.

Not to have "strange gods" means that we are not to love anyone or anything as much as we love God. We are to worship and adore him—that is, give him a special love which is owed to him alone, a love which acknowledges his supreme position above all creation.

In our love for God, we are to put nothing he has made before him. No creature is to be adored—that is, worshipped with that special love which we owe to God alone. Our love for or attachment to things God has made is not

15

wrong in itself—it is not wrong for a radio or a dog to have a place in our life. But these things must never compete with our love for God or with his plans for us. For example, if we love a stereo so much that we steal one, then we have put it before God.

There is a story from the Gospel which makes all this clear.

The Rich Young Man

A rich young man received an invitation from Our Lord himself to give up his riches and become a follower of Jesus. St. Mark tells us that Jesus looked at the young man and loved him, for the youth had always kept all of God's commandments and wanted to do even better. Jesus said to him: "There is one thing more you must do. Go and sell what you have and give to the poor; you will have treasure in Heaven. After that, come and follow me." (Mk 10:21)

But the young man turned away sadly and left Jesus because, as the Gospel says, he "had many possessions". He could not follow Jesus because he loved "creatures" too much. They may not have been the same creatures we

have—not radios or televisions or cars—but whatever they were, he could not find it in his heart to give them up. He missed the chance to follow Jesus because creatures were competing in his heart with love for God.

Therefore, there is danger in having many possessions, because they may turn our hearts from God. Our love for such things must be a "detached" love, a love that is ready to let go of things when God asks it of us.

Due Worship

In ages before Christ, the Hebrew people offered public sacrifice by slaughtering a valuable animal, like a lamb, upon an altar to honor God, to acknowledge him as Creator of all, and especially to make up for their sins.

The sacrifice of the Hebrew people pleased God but could never really make up for sin. As we know, the sin of Adam had closed the gates of Heaven. None of the many sacrifices offered by the Hebrews could change this. For sin offends God who is so great, and no offering of man alone, no matter how valuable, can make up for it.

Man's helplessness was not an obstacle to

God who wanted to save man. God himself became man and offered himself on the Cross as a fitting sacrifice, which was far more than enough to make up for all sins of all men. This sacrifice is renewed daily in every Mass around the world. The sacrifice of Jesus on the Cross is the greatest gift we can offer to God.

The sacrifice we offer in the Mass is the highest possible act of worship. It contains all that is necessary for giving due worship to God. In the Mass we acknowledge God as Creator, our Lord and Master. We offer thanks to him in gratitude for all he has given us. And, in recognition that we are dependent on him, we ask for all we need and for what will help others. Finally, we offer in the Mass the only thing that can make up for our sins and offenses. We offer the sacrifice of Jesus Christ on the Cross.

We can give God the love and worship we owe him when we participate in Holy Mass. Let's do so often!

Words to Know:

adore	idolatry
heresy	apostasy
worship	sacrifice
impiety	superstition
voluntary doubt	culpable ignorance

Q. 6 *What are we told to do by the First Commandment?*
The First Commandment commands us to be religious, that is, to believe in God and to love him, to adore him, and to serve him as the one true God, the Creator and Lord of all things.

Q. 7 *What does the First Commandment forbid?*
The First Commandment forbids impiety, superstition, and irreligious behavior; and in addition, apostasy, heresy, voluntary doubt, and culpable ignorance of the truths of faith.

"Bless the Lord, all you works of the Lord, Praise and exalt him above all forever."
(Daniel 3:57)

CHAPTER 3

Prayer—Hidden Treasure

Prayer is something required of us by the First Commandment. It is necessary for us to pray, and we must do so every day. God commanded us to pray, and he listens to our prayers.

Prayer is defined as the raising of the mind and heart to God. Our prayer is our communication with God. It may be done briefly or at length. We must have God in mind when we pray. We must think of something about him which moves us to love him. Then we can talk with him, adore him, tell him we are sorry for our sin, or ask him for things we need. One of the best ways to do this is to consider something Jesus said or did. Jesus, being man as well as God, can be pictured in the imagination; this helps to stir our heart, and then we can, for instance, make an act of faith, an act of hope, or an act of love.

There are two forms of prayer: vocal prayer and mental prayer. In the first we can use a set formula, like the Our Father, and it is spoken or recited. In the other we pray silently, with or without words; we just think about God and love him.

> The chief exercise of prayer is to speak to God and to hear God speak in the depths of your heart.
>
> — St. Francis de Sales

Our Need to Pray

Jesus strongly encourages us to pray. St. Luke records, "He [Jesus] told them a parable on the necessity of praying always and not losing heart. . . ." (Lk 18:1)

This means that we must pray even when we do not feel like it, as well as when we do; when unwanted thoughts interrupt our concentration; when worries tug us away from our thoughts about God, about Jesus, and about the saints. These interruptions are called "distractions". When they happen, we must return to prayer calmly and patiently. Distractions like this are not our fault. But if we begin to daydream and, after we realize it, continue to daydream instead of pray, we are at fault. If my mind wanders a hundred times, and I direct it back to prayer each time, there is no fault. In fact, there is great merit, because this is hard work and shows God that I love him and want to please him. By praying to God—asking for what we need, thanking him for what he has given us—we acknowledge that we are his creatures and that we are totally dependent on him.

Jesus assures us that our prayers will be answered. He says: "Ask, and you will re-

"Let my prayer arise before you, the lifting up of my hands like the evening sacrifice." *(Psalm 141)*

ceive. Seek, and you will find. Knock, and it will be opened to you.'' (Mt 7:7)

We will not, of course, get what is bad for us or what is really unnecessary. But God will always give us what is best for us.

Particular Prayers

There is a special prayer of the Church called the Liturgy of the Hours or the Divine Office. It is a prayer of praise and petition using the psalms and readings from Scripture and the writings of the saints. Certain members of the Church, such as priests, are required to pray the Divine Office every day, but all of us in the Church are invited to join in the Church's praise of God in this rich and beautiful form of prayer.

Another prayer specially recommended by the Church is the Rosary. For about eight hundred years, countless numbers of the faithful have made it part of their daily prayer. The Rosary is divided into mysteries, fifteen episodes in the lives of Jesus and Mary, and we are to think about these mysteries as we say the vocal prayers—mainly the Hail Marys. The prayers should be said slowly as our hearts are moved by what is in our minds. And what could be better suited to help us pray than scenes from the lives of Jesus and Mary?

*   *   *

A life of prayer is sometimes called the spiritual life or the devout life. Our spiritual life is the sum of all we do to reach Heaven, including our use of the sacraments and our good works. It is a way of growing; and the more we grow in prayer, the more joy, peace, and confidence we will have. A life of prayer makes us fully alive!

Jesus said: ''All this I tell you that my joy may be yours and your joy may be complete.'' (Jn 15:11)

Words to Know:

prayer   Divine Office (Liturgy of the Hours)

Form the habit of speaking to God as if you were alone with him, familiarly and with confidence and love, as to the dearest and most loving of friends. Speak to him often of your business, your plans, your troubles, your fears—of everything that concerns you. Talk with him confidently and frankly; for God does not often speak to a soul that does not speak to him.

— St. Alphonsus Liguori

Q. 8 *What is prayer?*

Prayer is a lifting of the soul to God, to know him better, to adore him, to thank him, and to ask him for what we need.

Q. 9 *How many kinds of prayer are there?*

There are two kinds of prayer: mental and vocal.

Q. 10 *What is mental prayer?*

Mental prayer is that which is said interiorly, with the mind and heart alone.

Q. 11 *What is vocal prayer?*

Vocal prayer is said by spoken words with the participation of the mind and heart.

Q. 12 *How should one pray?*

He who prays should do so reflecting that he stands in the presence of the infinite majesty of God and has need of his mercy: he should be humble, attentive, and devout in his prayer.

Q. 13 *Is it necessary to pray?*

Yes, it is necessary to pray, and to pray often, because God commands it, and because ordinarily he grants his graces only to those who pray.

Q. 14 *What things should we ask from God?*

We should ask from God his own glory, and for ourselves we should ask eternal life and graces, also for the temporal good, as Jesus Christ has taught us in the *Our Father*.

CHAPTER 4

Saints—They Made The Most of It

In this life we are all looking for the same thing: *happiness*. Saints are those who have found it. They are perfectly happy with God in Heaven. On earth they enjoyed a special closeness to God that brought them great happiness even in the midst of sufferings. But there is one thing we must always remember about the saints, and that is that they all started out just like each of us. What is more, each of us is called to be a saint too.

Many a saint, writing or speaking about his life, remembered being unhappy for years while he ignored God and followed the ways of the world. He might forget his unhappiness for awhile in seeking pleasure, but when the pleasure ended he was sadder than before. Then he had a change of heart, turned to God, and began a new life. Through prayer and the sacraments he practiced loving God, and he practiced loving his neighbors by doing good works. His old life of sin was over and done with.

The great St. Augustine wrote: "You have made us for yourself, O Lord, and our hearts are restless until they rest in you."

We can only be happy to the extent that we are in harmony with the will of God, that is, to the extent that we are doing what God wants.

Any distance from God, great or small, caused by sin, great or small, means that much unhappiness. The key to happiness, then, may be called "friendship with God" or doing God's will. The saints are close friends of God. This friendship brings them great joy, for we were made for friendship with God and nothing else can make up for that if we do not have it.

There is only one cure for the unhappy man, and that is for him to turn to God with all his heart. Nothing else can satisfy him.

Jesus calls sanctity, or happiness and holiness, the "Kingdom of God", and he compares true happiness to a merchant's search for fine pearls: "When he found one really valuable pearl, he went back and put up for sale all that he had and bought it." (Mt 13:46)

This is what the saints have done. In many cases they have completely changed their lives in order to conform to the gospel and be at peace with God. Now, after a happy life on earth, they enjoy the full and tremendous happiness of seeing God in Heaven.

Saints Victorious

We call the saints in Heaven the Church Triumphant, because they have grasped the

St. Charles Lwanga   St. John Bosco   St. Maximilian Kolbe

"To the saints honor must be paid as friends of Christ, as sons and heirs of God."

— St. John of Damascus

---

final prize which is God himself. God has given himself to them; he is theirs for all eternity. "Eternal life" doesn't just mean living forever; it means living *God's* life forever.

Intercessors

We should take advantage of the great power of the saints to intercede for us. "Intercede" means to speak up for us, to plead our case. We should pray to the saints and ask them to do this. They are called "intercessors"—those who intercede. When we pray to the saints we are honoring them, and in honoring them we honor God because we acknowledge that through God's grace they have been victorious over sin. We ask the saints to intercede for us because they are very dear friends of God. We should pray, particularly, to our patron saints, those for whom we have been named. And we should pray especially to the Blessed Virgin Mary, who is the greatest of the saints, given to us as our Mother by Jesus himself. We have many special prayers to Mary, but the best known is the "Hail Mary". We should also

pray to the good angels, although we know the names of only three of them: St. Michael the Archangel, St. Gabriel, whom God sent to the Blessed Virgin to ask her to become the mother of his Son, and St. Raphael. We should pray every day to our own guardian angel, for he is always with us to help us. In addition we should pray to our favorite saints, those for whom we feel a special attraction.

Besides asking the saints to intercede for us, we should study their lives so that we may learn from them how to attain our goal of Heaven. By imitating their virtuous lives we will find it easier to know and fulfill the will of God.

We should keep in mind that the saints are real people who are now with Jesus in Heaven. If we make friends with them today, they will remember us when we need them most.

The Blessed in Heaven

Those whom we honor by name as saints are those whom the Church has determined with complete certainty to be now in Heaven. There are many, many others in Heaven unknown to us whom we will meet when we get there.

How many saints are there, including all those of whom we do not now know? St. John, in the Book of Revelation, tells us of a vision of Heaven: "After this I saw before me a huge crowd which no one could count from every nation and race, people and tongue." (Rev 7:9)

This is comforting, but we should never take Heaven for granted. With St. Paul we must "run the race"; we must "fight the good fight". (2 Tim 4:6−7)

Words to Know:

Church Triumphant
patron saint   heroic virtue
saint   sanctity   intercessor

Q. 15 *Who are the saints?*
The saints are those who, by practicing the virtues to a heroic degree according to the teachings and example of Jesus Christ, have merited special glory in Heaven and also on earth, where, by the authority of the Church, they are publicly honored and called upon.

Q. 16 *If God hears him who prays well, why do we also pray to Our Lady, the angels, and the saints?*
We pray to Our Lady, the angels, and the saints because they are dear to God Our Lord and full of kindness toward us. Therefore they can help us in our request by their powerful intercession.

Q. 17 *Why are the angels, the saints, and Our Lady powerful intercessors with God?*
The angels and saints are powerful intercessors with God because they are his faithful servants and his beloved friends. Our Lady is the most powerful intercessor of all, because she is Mother of God. This is why we pray to her so frequently, and all the more because Jesus Christ left her to us as our Mother.

Q. 18 *What is the prayer that we use in a special way to invoke Our Lady?*
We invoke Our Lady especially with the Hail Mary.

CHAPTER 5

The Holy Name

"You shall not take the Name of the Lord your God in vain."

The Second Commandment forbids any lack of respect or due reverence toward God in the use of his most Holy Name, or toward any holy thing. Anyone who offends God by breaking this commandment is usually spiritually unwell, since no one who truly loves God would think of purposely misusing his Name. On the contrary, someone who loves God goes out of his way to bless God's Name and to make up for the times when others misuse his Name.

When Moses asked God for his Name, God called himself "I am who am". (Ex 3:14) That's all he would say. For the Jewish people this name was so great that they would not even say it but simply called God "the Lord".

What terrible foolishness, therefore, to misuse so great a Name!

***

There are different ways in which people violate the Second Commandment.

One way is called blasphemy. That is verbal abuse or scorn toward God himself or, by extension, to the Blessed Virgin, the saints, or holy things.

Another is by swearing false oaths. A false oath calls on God to witness to the truth of what we are saying when in fact we are lying. An oath in itself is not wrong. We may be involved in a legal proceeding which requires one. This is a good enough reason to take an oath; however, we should not take oaths invoking the divine Name without serious reason.

Obviously, a false oath is a very serious sin, since we are calling God, who is all Truth and all Justice, to witness to a lie.

Aside from the formality of a legal proceeding, it is common for people to use expressions like, "As God is my witness", or, "Honest to God". Spoken seriously, these are oaths and should not be used lightly. Said thoughtlessly or for trifles, they are swearing and should be avoided. (We must not confuse swearing with using bad language or cursing; using impure language may be against the Sixth Commandment and cursing against the Fifth.)

The Second Commandment also requires us to fulfill the vows and promises we have made. A vow is a solemn declaration committing oneself to do something. A vow in religion is a vow by which someone promises something for a religious reason. Religious brothers and sisters make vows of poverty, chastity, and obedience. A married couple makes a vow of fidelity.

Holy Things

We must not only respect God but must extend that respect to all those things that belong to God in a special way. We refer to our church as the house of God and a place of worship. It is a building consecrated to the glorification of God, and our behavior in church ought to express that.

All of the objects used for Mass, such as the altar, chalice, and paten, are holy because they are used in the highest form of worship. It is easy to see why we revere the Holy Bible, since it contains the word of God. And just as we treasure pictures and mementos of those we love, we also cherish crucifixes, religious medals, and pictures as reminders of God and his saints.

Certain people within the Church (the pope, bishops, priests, deacons, religious brothers and sisters) have consecrated their entire lives to God. Because they belong to God in a special way, we honor and respect them.

We express our love and reverence for God in the way we treat those things and people that belong to God.

Remember what God said to Moses from the burning bush: ''Moses! Moses! . . . Come no nearer. Remove the sandals from your feet, for the place where you stand is holy ground.'' (Ex 3:4−5)

Words to Know:

reverence   oath
blasphemy   vow

''O Lord, Our Lord, how glorious is your Name over all the earth.''
(Psalm 8:10)

Holy Name Society

Some parishes have an organization called the Holy Name Society. This society goes back to the nineteenth century. Its aim is to bring about due love and reverence for the Holy Name of God and Jesus Christ.

''From the rising of the sun to its setting, praised be the Name of the Lord!''

(Psalm 113)

"Young men and maidens, old men and children, praise the Name of the Lord, for his Name alone is exalted."
(Psalm 149)

Q. 19 *What is forbidden by the Second Commandment?*

The Second Commandment forbids us to dishonor the Name of God: that is, to use his Name without respect; to blaspheme God, the most holy Virgin, the saints, or holy things; and to swear oaths that are false, not necessary, or wrong in any way.

Q. 20 *What is an oath?*

An oath is calling upon God as witness for what is declared or promised. A person who swears falsely offends God seriously, for God is holiness and truth itself.

Q. 21 *Is blasphemy a serious sin?*

Yes, blasphemy is a serious sin because it is injury and scorn toward God and his saints.

Q. 22 *What are we ordered to do by the Second Commandment?*

The Second Commandment orders us to maintain always a reverence for the Name of God and to fulfill the vows and promises to which we have bound ourselves.

Q. 23 *What is a vow?*

A vow is a promise made to God of some good that is pleasing to him, to which we bind ourselves for a religious reason.

HALLOWED BE THY NAME

CHAPTER 6

The Lord's Day

Time is precious. Most people would agree on that. But this does not mean the same thing to everyone. Most people think that they never have enough time to do what *they* want to do.

So when God asks for some of our time for himself, people react differently. Some are so happy to give time to God that they are grateful for every opportunity. Others can't be bothered. They are shortsighted, for all men eventually run out of time, while God alone possesses a world without end which he wants to share with us. As we say in the prayer:

Glory be to the Father and to the Son and to the Holy Spirit; as it was in the beginning, is now, and ever shall be, *world without end. Amen.*

The Third Commandment tells us to give one day a week to God.

"Remember to keep holy the Lord's Day."

And it is written:

Six days you may labor and do all your work, but the seventh day is the Sabbath of the Lord, your God. (Ex 20:8−10)

The Sabbath is a *holy* day, which, like anything holy, is consecrated or dedicated to God, set aside for him. God himself says that in six days he made the world and on the seventh he rested.

The Jewish people observe the Sabbath on Saturday, the last day of the week and the day on which God rested. But Christians observe Sunday instead, the day Jesus Christ, our Savior, rose from the dead. We give him this day, this entire day, to show that we recognize who he is and to honor and glorify him. Each Sunday is like Easter; we are celebrating the Resurrection of the Lord and his triumph over death.

Making it a Holy Day

We owe God a double debt as Creator and Redeemer, and we make some repayment—at least a small amount—by making Sunday a really holy day.

First of all, we put aside our work, which has had our attention all week long, and we turn our eyes to God, because although work is very good and necessary, it is nevertheless a concern with what God has made—creation— and not with God who made it.

For this reason we are commanded not to do any unnecessary work on Sundays and Holy Days. Our jobs and unnecessary schoolwork should be set aside. There are some jobs which make it necessary for some people to work on Sunday, such as doctors and nurses, policemen, bus drivers, farmers, and others who must work because of economic necessity; but most jobs can and should be put aside on Sunday.

The Third Commandment demands of us

some form of external worship, not just internal or private worship. This is because our entire being is subject to God, both body and soul. We need to demonstrate this external worship publicly as a witness to the whole community that God has first place in our lives. God desires that our devotion be visible; he wants to be worshipped in broad daylight for all the world to see. Private devotion cannot take the place of this. If we omit outward worship together as a community, our faith will weaken and we may fall away from God.

The principal tribute we offer to God on the Lord's Day is participation in the Holy Sacrifice of the Mass, because it is the greatest act of worship. For a Catholic, Sunday without Holy Mass is not a holy day. To miss Mass on Sunday is a mortal sin—unless, of course, there is a serious reason, such as sickness or lack of transportation or a need to work, that excuses us.

We must always remember that although Mass on Sunday is an obligation we are bound to, it is also a blessed opportunity for us. Anyone making a sincere effort to live the gospel will go not only to Holy Mass but to Holy Communion as well. Not to go to Sunday Mass is to cut ourselves off from the sacraments and the grace which flows through them from Jesus to us. For Jesus says: "I am the vine, you are the branches. He who lives in me, and I in him, will produce abundantly, for apart from me you can do nothing." (Jn 15:5)

Missing Mass on Sunday is a great misfortune. It is also a great pity to go to Mass regularly but stay away from the sacraments of Penance and Holy Communion. This would be a sign that Sunday Mass is just a duty, that there is no life in our observance, and that we do not understand much about the life of the spirit or taste much of the goodness of the Lord.

***

There is great disrespect for the Lord's Day in our society, and it is growing all the time. It has always been understood that certain stores and certain services, such as hospitals and the police, have to be available on Sunday; but now we see people buying all sorts of unnecessary things in department stores that hum with business on this day, as if it were a day like any other. It is a sign that many people have lost touch with the spiritual side of life. If they were aware that life is not just something to be lived any old way, but a time to become like Jesus, then we would not have such abuses.

Day of Rest

Besides being a day to attend Mass, Sunday is supposed to be a day of joy and refreshment. Wholesome fun is a wonderful ingredient of holiness. We may take time for reading good books, for more personal prayer and private devotions, works of charity, sports, hobbies, and real rest.

Let's use our imagination! As Mother Teresa of Calcutta says, let's do "something beautiful for God"! Let's really make Sunday a holy day.

"This is the day the Lord has made; Let us rejoice and be glad in it."

(Psalm 118)

Holy Days of Obligation

In addition to the obligation of Sunday Mass, there are holy days of obligation, days which have the same obligation as Sundays. The universal Church has ten special holy days that may fall on days other than Sundays. They are:

- Solemnity of Mary the Mother of God—January 1
- Epiphany—January 6
- Feast of St. Joseph—March 19
- Ascension Thursday—forty days after Easter
- Corpus Christi—first Thursday after Pentecost
- Feast of SS. Peter and Paul—June 29
- The Assumption of Mary—August 15
- All Saints' Day—November 1
- Immaculate Conception—December 8
- Christmas—December 25

In certain countries attendance at Mass is not obligatory on all these holy days. In the United States some are celebrated on Sunday and only six others *require* our attendance at Mass. These are the Solemnity of Mary, Ascension Thursday, Assumption, All Saints' Day, Immaculate Conception, and Christmas. However, if it is convenient for us to attend Mass on the other holy days and special feasts, we will want to do so.

Words to Know:

Sabbath   holy days of obligation

Q. 24 *What are we ordered to do by the Third Commandment?*
The Third Commandment orders us to honor God on Sundays and holy days by acts of external worship, and for Catholics the most important of these is Holy Mass.

Q. 25 *Why must we do acts of external worship?*
It is not sufficient to adore God internally in the heart, but we must also give him external worship as commanded, because we are subject to God in our entire being, both soul and body. Furthermore, we are bound to give good example. And finally, if we were to omit external worship we might lose our religious spirit.

Q. 26 *Are we required to hear Mass?*
We are required to hear Mass on Sunday and on the holy days of obligation. But it is good also to attend Mass frequently, in order to participate in the greatest act of religion, the one which is most pleasing to God and most meritorious to us.

Q. 27 *What is prohibited by the Third Commandment?*
The Third Commandment forbids us to do ''servile works'' on Sundays and holy days.

Q. 28 *What kind of works are called ''servile''?*
''Servile works'' is the name given to physical labor and those activities that would hinder renewal of soul and body on the Lord's Day.

CHAPTER 7

The Cross and True Riches

The path through life to Heaven is often compared to climbing a mountain, and the mountain-top is Heaven, God's holy mountain. In Psalm 43, the pilgrim on life's journey cries out to God:

O send forth your light and your truth;
let these be my guide!
Let them bring me to your holy mountain,
to the place where you dwell.

Christ our Savior offers us a way that will lead to peace, joy, and our final goal of total happiness with God. The way that leads to this wonderful state of perfection, or holiness, is based on Jesus' words: "Whoever wishes to be my follower must deny his very self, take up his cross each day, and follow in my steps." (Lk 9:23)

Self-denial may mean doing something we would rather not do or refusing some pleasure we would like: for example, taking time to help your brother with his fractions or giving up dessert sometimes. An example on a deeper level is giving your schoolwork your best effort, although it may not be easy and you may have to give up much of your free time to do it. Your schoolwork (or perhaps a particular subject) may take on the nature of a cross, especially if it is difficult.

Now we have come to a great mystery—the doctrine of the Cross. It is the principal sign of Christianity. As a result of original sin, it is necessary for us to put to death in ourselves a certain way of living which St. Paul calls "the old man" and to put on "the new man", Jesus.

The old man is Adam, who misused the gifts of God and so brought sin and disorder into the world. As you know, this sin is passed on to us as Adam's children. We are born in the state of original sin. Through Baptism we are given the life of grace, but original sin has left in us many wounds and disorders. These wounds can only be healed by a lifetime of right living, prayer, and self-denial.

This is not always easy. When Jesus asks us to love our enemy and to do good to those who hurt us, he is not asking us to do something that comes naturally or easily. But, by the power of God, it is not impossible. For with God "all things are possible". (Mt 19:26)

The Cross sums up all the things which, naturally speaking, are most distasteful to us, such as a penance we choose for ourselves or a suffering that God allows in our life—perhaps an enemy at school or some sickness—permitted for our good or the good of others, though we may not be able to see it at the time.

Bearing the crosses (that is, trials and dif-

"God loves a cheerful giver."

(2 Corinthians 9:7)

ficulties) which we do not choose but which come to us anyhow in the course of life is a most perfect kind of self-denial, more pleasing to God than the acts of self-denial we choose for ourselves. For in all things it is most perfect to accept the will of God, especially when we do not like it very much. Jesus' entire life was one of obedience to the will of the Father, no matter how hard it was or what it required of him, even his death. ''Father, if it is your will, take this cup from me; yet not my will but yours be done.'' (Lk 22:42)

And why are we willing to set out on such a way of life? In following the example of Jesus we are showing our love for God by willingly and, yes, even cheerfully accepting whatever he permits.

Fast and Abstinence

We are encouraged to choose some penance for ourselves. To help us, the Church requires us to fast and to abstain from certain foods on penitential days. To abstain, in this case, means not to eat meat. If we are fourteen years old or more, we must abstain from meat on Ash Wednesday and Good Friday.

In the United States, the bishops have further declared abstinence from meat on all Fridays of Lent. In other seasons, Friday remains a day of penance on which we are supposed to practice some kind of self-denial, and the bishops advise us to make Friday a day of abstinence all year round.

Fasting, in general, means not eating at all. When the Church requires us to fast, however, it means that only one full meal a day should be eaten. In addition, two smaller meals may be taken, but those taken together should not equal another full meal. In the Church, there are two days of required fasting: Ash Wednesday and Good Friday. This applies to anyone eighteen to sixty years old.

Penitential Seasons

Advent and Lent are special seasons in the Church year in which we are reminded to renew our spirit. They are called penitential seasons.

Advent begins four Sundays before Christmas and is a season of special preparation for the birth of Christ. The Church suggests that we do some form of penance as part of this preparation.

The season of Lent begins six and a half weeks before Easter and is a season of preparation for the Passion, death, and Resurrection of the Lord. Just as Jesus fasted for forty days, we too take on some penance during Lent to make up for our sins and to prepare our hearts to celebrate the great Easter feast.

''When you fast, you are not to look glum as the hypocrites do. They change the appearance of their faces so that others may see they are fasting. . . . When you fast, see to it that you groom your hair and wash your face. In that way no one can see you are fasting but your Father who is hidden; and your Father who sees what is hidden will reward you.''

(Matthew 6:16–18)

St. Paul compares the spiritual life to a race and the Christian to an athlete.

Like an athlete, the Christian is asked to practice certain spiritual exercises. If an athlete will give up a great deal just to train for a race, how much more should we Christians be ready to practice self-denial for the sake of the Kingdom of God!

Besides, what the athlete gives up in training is not always so great, and his self-discipline is often very satisfying, invigorating, and enjoyable. His muscle tone, increased skill, and sense of well-being make it all worthwhile.

It is the same way with the Kingdom of God. The Cross does not always stand for something great and awful. It can include many little things which make up our daily lives, such as not having our way, forgiving an unkind word, turning from fun to duties at the proper time, not overeating and the like. Nor are we expected to make life one big penance with no pleasures. After all, it is God who created the things in which we find pleasure. But, like a good athlete, we must keep an eye on the coach—Jesus—and not forget ourselves and break training.

Penance, therefore, makes up for past sin and helps prevent future sin. It helps eliminate those things that take us away from God or are obstacles to our final goal—union with God in his Kingdom.

Words to Know:

self-denial	penance	fasting
abstinence	Advent	Lent

Rules of Fast and Abstinence

— The days and times of penance for the universal Church are each Friday of the whole year and the season of Lent.

— Abstinence and fasting are to be observed on Ash Wednesday and Good Friday. Abstinence is to be observed on all the Fridays during Lent.

— The law of abstinence binds those who have completed their fourteenth year. The law of fasting binds those who have attained their twenty-first year, until the beginning of their sixtieth year.

Dearest Lord, teach me to be generous;
teach me to serve you as you deserve to be served—
to give and not to count the cost,
to fight and not to heed the wounds,
to toil and not to seek for rest,
to labor and not to ask any reward
except that of knowing that I do your holy will.

—St. Ignatius Loyola

CHAPTER 8

In the Heart of the Family

We sometimes see elderly people with their children who are themselves approaching old age. No matter how old the parents are, no matter how old the children, the law of the Lord remains:

"Honor your father and mother."

Even without the Fourth Commandment we would be able to see that we have certain obligations toward our parents, for we would never have existed without them. They are special; they have given us life. This gift is so great that there is no way to repay them completely.

To see what is required of us by the Fourth Commandment, we need to look at family relations. Without children, husband and wife make a marriage; with a child, they make a family. The child is an extension of their love for each other and is included in their love. The relation of parent to child is a lasting one, no matter how old one is. It is from his parents that a child learns what love is, and in that love the child is able to learn that God is also his loving Father.

Each child is a precious gift from God. But along with the blessing of a child there are many duties and responsibilities that parents must take on. God gives them the authority and duty to maintain good order in the home, to provide food and clothing, to educate, and to tend to the welfare of each member of their family.

Now, the commandment tells us to "honor" our parents. To honor means to hold in high regard, to respect, and to love. A child honors his parents when he respects their authority over him. This also includes respecting and obeying those whom our parents place in authority over us, such as a teacher or scout leader.

It is part of God's plan to provide for the well-being and development of children to place them under the loving authority of their parents. And so obedience to that authority is required.

With the years, children may discover faults and weaknesses in their parents; in God's plan children can sometimes be a powerful force for good and a source of grace for their parents. Prayer and sacrifice for the welfare of one's parents are always blessed by God.

As children get older they need less care and direction until they reach a point at which they are able to order their own lives. It is only reasonable, then, that the relationship between parent and child should gradually change. Obedience turns into respect for the wisdom of our parents until we reach an age at which we are no longer bound by obedience but still gratefully accept our parents' advice.

Anyone who honors his parents will, when

he grows older, look after their needs. In this regard, life is like a seesaw with the heavier end holding up the other. As a youngster, the child sits at the end upraised, with mother and father holding down the other. Many years later, the child holds the seesaw down while the elderly parents receive the care and attention. They cared for us; now we care for them.

The Bible teaches: ''My son, take care of your father when he is old; grieve him not as long as he lives.'' (Sir 3:12)

And God promises to bless those who keep the Fourth Commandment:

Honor your father and your mother, that you may have a long life in the land which the Lord, your God, is giving you. (Ex 20:12)

The Family Today

In his Apostolic Exhortation *Familiaris Consortio*, ''The Role of the Christian Family in the Modern World'', Pope John Paul II singled out the family as the main target in the renewal of modern society. The family is so important that we cannot hope to survive as a society unless family life is healthy and strong. This means that strong love among all the members must unite the whole family and make it holy.

The Holy Family, Jesus, Mary, and Joseph, was united with that holy love. We should look to them as our model for family life.

There are many forces in our society that weaken the bonds of family life and even threaten to destroy it. The Christian family will survive only with renewed love for God and neighbor. We must pray together for our own families and for the family in general. Where there is no prayer, there will be no family unity and peace. With prayer, we can hope for the blessings of family happiness on earth and reunion in our heavenly home.

Words to Know:

honor

Q. 29 *What does the Fourth Commandment order us to do?*
The Fourth Commandment orders us to love, respect, and obey our parents and whoever holds authority over us.

Q. 30 *What does the Fourth Commandment forbid?*
The Fourth Commandment forbids us to offend or disobey our parents and superiors in authority.

Father, it is your commandment that we should honor our father and mother; hear the prayers I offer you for my parents. Grant them many years on earth, and keep them healthy in mind and body. Bless their work and all they do. Give them back a hundredfold whatever they have done for me. Inspire them with your love, and help them to fulfill your holy law. One day, may I be their comfort and support, so that, having enjoyed their affection on earth, I may have the joy of being with them forever in your home in Heaven. Through Christ Our Lord. *Amen*.

CHAPTER 9

Citizenship—Rights and Duties

As members of a family we see how we are dependent on others and others depend on us. We become more aware that the happiness and well-being of all men are connected. Men come together and form larger societies. So we are members not only of a family but also of a state. Our parents exercise certain rightful authority over us, and so does the state. The state's authority over us is from God. St. Paul tells us: "Let every person be subject to the governing authorities. For there is no authority except from God. . . . Therefore he who resists the authorities resists what God has appointed." (Rom 13:1-2)

The state has the authority to make just laws and regulations to govern its citizens. The purpose of the state is to promote and preserve the welfare of all the members of its society. Jesus never denied the rights of the state; he tells us to give to God what is God's, and to Caesar (the state) what is Caesar's.

The state can never demand something of us which is in violation of God's law. If it did, the state would be denying its own authority, since that authority is from God.

As you probably already know, there are different kinds of government. Now, God has never told us that one particular type of government is better than another. There can

be several legitimate and good ways to govern a nation.

Good Citizens

Just as the state has certain rights and duties, so do we as citizens. As Christians we must be exemplary citizens, obeying all just laws and regulations, paying taxes to support the government, and when necessary defending our nation from attack.

Patriotism is the virtue of love of one's country. This virtue is in keeping with Christianity because it is natural and good for us to love our fatherland. But patriotism is not mere flag-waving. It is dedication to the promotion of the true welfare of the whole country and its citizens.

As citizens, the health and well-being of the state is our concern. We must use our influence to make it a just state. The Christian input in society is essential. If there is an unjust practice or immoral law, then we must do all in our power to overturn it. We must work within the structure of our government to reestablish justice and to make it secure.

Just because the state declares that some action is legal, it does not necessarily follow that it is moral. We have today the grave evil of "legalized abortion". The state has declared a seriously immoral and evil act to be acceptable and "within the law". Not only are we forbidden to support such a declaration but we are also required to do all in our power to overturn such a law. We are not allowed to tolerate such violations of the law of God. "Better for us to obey God than men!" (Acts 5:29)

Across Boundaries

As followers of Christ we must not isolate ourselves within our own nation. We must be concerned about the needs of all people. Many people and nations are oppressed and deprived of basic human rights by severe poverty or by lack of freedom. Just as there are different forms of good governments, so there are governments that are bad and threaten the well-being of their citizens. Wealthier and stronger countries have a responsibility to aid these oppressed nations. As citizens we must encourage our government to do what is possible to help people in need.

Above all we must remember to pray for our country and its leaders.

Q. 31 *Why are we obliged to obey superiors in authority?*
We are obliged to obey superiors in authority because "there is no authority except from God; . . . as a consequence, the man who opposes authority rebels against the ordinance of God." (Rom 13:1-2)

St. Thomas More

In the year 1535 Sir Thomas More was beheaded by order of the King of England and his court of law. Thomas More had been friend to King Henry the Eighth and had even held the office of Lord Chancellor, second in power to the King. What had Sir Thomas More done that caused his one-time friend and ruler to have him put to death? He had chosen to obey God's law rather than man's.

King Henry the Eighth had declared himself to be the supreme head of the Church in England. Thomas More knew that such a declaration was a violation of the law of God, and so he would not accept it, even if his refusal meant death.

St. Thomas More had been a great statesman and had dedicated himself to the service of his king and country. But he knew that God's law was above the King's, and so he was willing to die ''the King's good servant, but God's first''. For suffering this martyrdom, Thomas More has been declared a saint by the Church.

CHAPTER 10

Church Authority— Our Fathers in Faith

Besides our parents and the state there is another society that has authority over us and demands our obedience and allegiance. That is the Catholic Church as founded on earth by Jesus.

It is Jesus who gave to the Church its mission to save souls, to teach all men the truths of the Faith, and to govern the Church as a body. Establishing the Church was the means Jesus chose to remain with us always and to lead us to his Heavenly Kingdom, our final goal.

The Vicar of Christ

It is Jesus who is the Head or Ruler of his Church. He is the one who has given the authority to the pope to rule the Church on his behalf. It was to St. Peter, the first pope, that Jesus said: ''I will give you the keys of the Kingdom of Heaven, and whatever you bind on earth shall be bound in Heaven, and whatever you loose on earth shall be loosed in Heaven.'' (Mt 16:19)

Including our present Pope, John Paul II, there have been 264 popes, and the authority of St. Peter has been passed on to each one down to our own day.

The mission of the Church is to preach the gospel and lead all people to holiness. The pope is chiefly responsible for seeing that this mission is accomplished. It is for this purpose that the pope and bishops, as successors of the apostles, have the authority to make the precepts or laws and disciplines of the Church.

A bishop is the chief authority in his own diocese as long as he governs in union with the pope. He delegates some of his authority to the priests of his diocese. The priests, the bishops, and the pope are all instruments of Christ, who governs his Church through these ordained ministers.

The Church is carefully governed so that it may be clearly recognized by the unity of its faith and worship.

Unity of Faith

To make sure that the Faith is taught correctly and the gospel preached to all without error, the pope has the authority to declare just what is to be taught. He answers moral questions and addresses himself to any current problem which affects the lives of Christians. The pope does this in his speeches, encyclicals, letters, and declarations. The bishops do the same in their dioceses, usually through pastoral letters which are read to us in Church.

One in the Sacraments

Since it is through the sacraments that the Church fulfills its role in sanctifying men, it is necessary that they be administered in a consistent way in all times and places. It is the Church that determines what is required to receive each sacrament: for example, how old a person must be and what the accompanying ceremony should include. The Church also sets the requirements for becoming and remaining a member of the Church.

Holy Mother Church

The Church is often referred to as our Holy Mother Church. This denotes the attitude we should have toward the Church and her leaders. Like all mothers, the Church exists to give us life and to provide for our well-being and development until we reach our final goal. We should have great reverence and love for the Church, because Jesus gave us the Church as a sign of his love for us.

Words to Know:

Vicar of Christ   precepts

Q. 32 *Why does the Church have the authority to make laws and precepts?*
The Church has the authority to make laws and precepts because it has received this authority from Jesus Christ through his apostles. Thus he who disobeys the Church disobeys God himself.

Q. 33 *Who can make laws and precepts in the Church?*
In the Church the pope and the bishops as successors of the apostles can make laws and precepts, for Jesus Christ said to them: ''He who hears you hears me. And he who rejects you rejects me.'' (Lk 10:16)

Precepts of the Church

1. To keep holy the day of the Lord's Resurrection; to worship God by participating in Mass every Sunday and holy day of obligation; to avoid those activities that would hinder renewal of soul and body on the Lord's day.
2. To lead a sacramental life; to receive Holy Communion frequently and the Sacrament of Penance regularly—minimally, to receive the Sacrament of Penance at least once a year (annual confession is obligatory only if serious sin is involved); minimally also, to receive Holy Communion at least once a year, between the First Sunday of Lent and Trinity Sunday.
3. To study Catholic teaching in preparation for the Sacrament of Confirmation, to be confirmed, and then to continue to study and advance the cause of Christ.
4. To observe the marriage laws of the Church; to give religious training, by example and word, to one's children; to use parish schools and catechetical programs.
5. To strengthen and support the Church—one's own parish community and parish priests, the worldwide Church, and the pope.
6. To do penance, including abstaining from meat and fasting from food on the appointed days.
7. To join the missionary spirit and apostolate of the Church.

CHAPTER 11

Respect Life

The Fifth Commandment is:

"You shall not kill."

Man is a creature composed of body and soul. Some people go about their business as if they had never heard of the soul. It is also possible to find some, though today they are fewer in number, who look down on the body and almost try to live like angels, who are pure spirits. The truth is that both body and soul are essential to the human being. And, though parted by death, the body and the soul are destined to be reunited at the resurrection on the Last Day.

Because we have a soul we are called to share in God's life. We call this supernatural life, because it is above our natural life here on earth.

The Fifth Commandment gives us the responsibility to care for both the natural and supernatural life that God has given to us and all men.

Right to Life

Since God is the giver of life, no man or group of men has the right to take innocent human life. To do so is murder. And murder is a serious crime and a very serious sin, a mortal sin. If we look around, we can see that many people think they can take the matter of life and death into their own hands. Many people ignore or accept the murder of millions of unborn babies in our own nation and around the world. An estimated fifty million unborn babies are killed every year.

Another area where there is a weakening of respect for human life is what is called euthanasia, or "mercy killing". It is never justified. A sick, elderly person must be given the normal or ordinary treatment to keep him or her alive. To do otherwise would be murder. Extraordinary treatment is another matter—it is not obligatory.

These days there is more and more pressure for euthanasia from many quarters. Men are taking the beginning and the end of life into their own hands.

The Fifth Commandment makes it clear that it is wrong to take innocent life. Some people maintain that all killing is wrong and never allowable, no matter what the reasons. But there are certain situations in which killing is not the same thing as murder. The most obvious examples of this are the taking of life in self-defense, capital punishment, and just wars. The Church has never condemned these acts as murder. But since every act of taking human life is a serious matter, we must always look to the Church for guidance in this area.

Murder is not the only violation of the Fifth Commandment. It would be a mortal sin to injure someone seriously by careless driving. It is wrong *not to care* whether our actions may injure others.

Suicide, the act of killing oneself, is always wrong. If someone commits suicide without full knowledge and consent, however, his responsibility before God is lessened. God alone is the Master of our lives, and we are too precious in his sight to toss our lives away. But it is wrong, too, not to take proper care of ourselves, with proper diet, exercise, and rest. We should avoid risking our lives by doing foolish stunts when we are egged on by a dare or a desire to show off. We should protect ourselves from disease by sensible habits of cleanliness and dress. We should avoid impatience and carelessness that may lead to accident or injury.

Intemperate eating and drinking is a sin that can harm the body; so is the improper use of medicines and other drugs. All in all, taking a little less food and drink than we want is a small but sensible restraint on our bodies and an excellent form of self-denial. As we have seen, some self-denial is a necessary part of Christian living.

Words to Know:

murder   suicide

"Anyone who hates his brother is a murderer, and you know that eternal life abides in no murderer's heart."

(1 John 3:15)

Q. 34 *What does the Fifth Commandment forbid?*
The Fifth Commandment forbids us to harm the life, either natural or spiritual, of our neighbor as well as of ourselves. It prohibits murder, suicide, unjustified fighting, curses, and scandal.

Q. 35 *Why is suicide a sin?*
Suicide is a sin, like murder, because God alone is Master of our life, just as he alone is Master of our neighbor's life.

CHAPTER 12

Charity toward All

The law of love—"Love your neighbor as yourself"—is closely connected to the rules that arise from the Fifth Commandment. We have seen many striking and violent offenses against this commandment. There are other more common offenses in which persons are not hurt physically but harm is done. Such actions are far from Christian.

Goodwill

Christ preached goodwill toward all, friends and enemies alike. This is what is involved in the injunction: "Love your enemies." It is hard enough not to strike back when we are hurt; it is even harder to respond with love.

But how do we know if we love our enemies? Do we have to love them with our feelings? Do I have to *feel* this love for my enemy? Not necessarily. We will not be held accountable for the absence of such feeling, but we are responsible for *goodwill*.

I will know whether I love my enemy if I wish him well. We must wish well to everyone; my will, where I wish others well or ill, is the center of my love. I may not *like* my enemy, but if I wish him well and treat him well, I am fulfilling Christ's words, "Love your enemies."

One thing that gets in the way of goodwill is anger. When we lose our tempers, we say things and do things to get back at others, to

hurt them. How terrible, then, the gift of speech can be! We can make it a weapon by yelling at someone, calling someone names, or cursing. All these things come under the Fifth Commandment, which prohibits deliberate injury to another human being in any way.

Closely linked to anger is hatred. To hate someone is to wish evil to someone, or even to wish that he did not exist! It may be conceived in the heat of anger but persist even when the feelings have cooled down because, like love, it is willed, although it is the very opposite of love. This is ill will, a wish that another person be hurt and suffer, perhaps even be killed.

St. John wrote: "Anyone who hates his brother is a murderer." (1 Jn 3:15) Indeed, we can have our neighbor dead and buried in our minds without ever doing anything to him, but because of our hatred we are murderers!

All this can start, perhaps, because we lost our tempers and began to nurture ill will. The danger of anger is that we do things blindly, unaware of the evil in our thoughts, careless of the bitter enmity we may provoke with our stinging words, perhaps stirred even to the point of physical violence.

Jesus left no doubt about the sinfulness of anger when he said in the Sermon on the Mount:

You have heard the commandment imposed on your forefathers, "You shall not commit murder; every murderer shall be liable to judgment." What I say to you is: everyone who grows angry with his brother shall be liable to judgment; any man who uses abusive language toward his brother shall be answerable. . . . (Mt 5:21–22)

When someone has hurt us in some way, we are required to refrain not only from striking back but also from harboring ill feeling toward him. We must do something positive. Jesus says: "Love your enemies, do good to to those who hate you; bless those who curse you and pray for those who maltreat you." (Lk 6:27–28)

And St. Paul wrote: "Bless your persecutors; bless and do not curse them. Never repay injury with injury." (Rom 12:14–15)

Here is a thought which can take a lot of the sting out of hard words and bad treatment: try offering the pain to God for the salvation of the one who hurts you. No matter how you feel, surely you would like to see your enemy in Heaven someday.

In addition, if you get the opportunity, show respect and consideration to your enemy. Suddenly you may see things through the eyes of Jesus. How many times he was insulted! No doubt he felt the pain, like every other man—perhaps even more—but he knew that the souls of those who insulted him were wonderful creations and that no matter how bad they were, they were continually being called to a new life of grace.

Not all anger is wrongful. There is such a thing as *just anger*; for instance, when Jesus chased the moneylenders from the Temple or

when he rebuked hypocrites. Righteous anger can help us to stand up for the rights of oppressed persons or come to the defense of those suffering unjust aggression. It may help us to speak up for someone who isn't getting his rights—ourselves or others. Finally, a holy anger may motivate us to fight for a very important cause—like working in the pro-life movement to end the evil of legalized abortion.

Scandal

There is a special case of bad will which Jesus condemned with utmost severity: scandal. It is a fully conscious and deliberate bad example or encouragement meant to lead another person into sin. It is probably the worst of all sins because it endangers someone else's eternal destiny. There can be no greater lack of charity.

Any sinful act could lead another into sin, but anything said or done with the knowledge that it may weaken the faith or destroy the spiritual life of another is scandal. The person who gives scandal is responsible for all the sins into which others are led. Jesus said:

It would be better for anyone who leads astray one of these little ones who believe in me to be drowned with a millstone around his neck in the depths of the sea. (Mt 18:6)

Forgive Us, as We Forgive Others

On the Cross Jesus prayed to his Father to "forgive them, for they know not what they are doing". As followers of Christ we must be willing to forgive those who hurt us. And we must also govern our thoughts and actions so that we do not injure other people physically or spiritually.

Words to Know:

scandal   cursing

"Let all bitterness and wrath and anger and clamor and slander be put away from you, with all malice, and be kind to one another, tenderhearted, forgiving one another, as God in Christ forgave you."   *(Ephesians 4:31—32)*

Q. 36 *What is scandal?*
Scandal is the leading of others into sin by any of our actions.

Q. 37 *What are we ordered to do by the Fifth Commandment?*
The Fifth Commandment orders us to be of good will toward all, including our enemies, and to make up for any bodily or spiritual evil done to our neighbor.

CHAPTER 13

The Sacred Flame

All men were made by God in his image and likeness. And all of us are known and loved by God as distinct individuals. It is this special relation each of us has to God that is the foundation of our dignity as persons.

Everyone has this dignity as a child of God, and so every individual is worthy of our respect, for each person is made by God to be loved by him and to have God's life within. We ourselves have this dignity, of course, and so we must also have respect for ourselves—self-respect.

To maintain our self-respect and respect for others we have to do what we know is right and avoid what we know is wrong. To do this we need to develop our self-control and overcome our weaknesses.

The Sixth and Ninth Commandments,

"You shall not commit adultery"
and
"You shall not covet your neighbor's wife",

demand from us that respect which we are to have for ourselves and for others, and in a special way for those things that belong to married life and the family.

Be Fruitful

When a seed is planted in the earth there are certain laws that govern its development, and if the conditions are right it grows into a specific plant, whether it is a sunflower or an olive tree. Then it will produce seeds after its own kind which will propagate the species—that is, reproduce or multiply. God finds this very good; it is the way he designed things.

Animals propagate as well. Like the flowers, when conditions are right everything happens according to certain laws and there is no misuse of these powers. We don't have to preach self-control to plants and animals because they act through instinct.

But man is different. Like plants and animals, he reproduces and multiplies and fills the earth. This is what God wants, for Scripture says:

> God created man in his image; in the divine image he created him; male and female he created them. God blessed them, saying: "Be fruitful and multiply; fill the earth. . . ." (Gen 1:27–28)

But, unlike the rest of visible creation, man does not multiply blindly, following the seasons, like plants, or by instinct, like animals. These creatures are not free to make decisions about their reproductive powers. Man *is* free. This is an aspect of man's dignity. It is also a possible source of abuse.

Man may have very powerful urges, but he is not led blindly by his instincts. The plant or animal does not have to trouble itself about the proper use of its powers. For man, though, their use is not a matter of "instinct". Man is called to cooperate with God in a plan that is not recorded in his genes or in his blood but is revealed by God in his Commandments—specifically, the Sixth and Ninth Commandments.

Many people look upon these two Commandments as restrictions; but we can think about them in the following way. The seed that becomes a sunflower is guided to this fulfillment by a biochemical blueprint invented by God. And though we do not see it, God who holds the sacred flame of *all* life has a blueprint for our fulfillment too, and he alone is wise enough to guide the use of man's reproductive powers. If he can lead the sunflower to full beauty from a seed, then he can lead a man to fullness of life by the laws he has given us, though we may see only a little of his plan.

When you are about to plant a seed and water it, you do not have to remind it to trust God; the seed knows all that, so to speak. It is *man* who needs to be reminded to trust God!

Laws of Life

All this is said to point out the proper beauty and value of the human reproductive powers. The Sixth Commandment guides us in our actions, the Ninth in our thoughts and desires. It is important to remember that all our actions start in our mind, and so we should see the importance of properly directing our thoughts and desires.

Put simply, the pleasures and joys of human sexuality are reserved for marriage. Any use of these powers outside of marriage is a serious sin. God plans to give those who marry an actual share in the creation of a new human being; God creates the soul and the human parents help fashion the body. Does it seem unreasonable, then, for God to surround the use of these powers with laws to ensure their rightful use? Sexuality is something central to our human nature; isn't it important to use our sexuality according to the will of God, who created and loves our nature?

The love between a man and a woman,

made fruitful and blessed by God in marriage, lovingly brings a new child into a family, where he will have the attention and devotion of both father and mother. It is to assure such conditions for children that God has designed human sexuality to be enjoyed only in marriage, and then only in the proper way. Society is filled to overflowing with the problems and evils and afflictions caused by disregard for God's wise guidance and authority.

The proper use or control of our sexual powers is called chastity, which is a virtue or good habit. It requires that we practice self-denial and self-control. A chaste person will avoid anything that might be a temptation to sin, such as indecent books and movies. Our purity is something to be protected. To safeguard it we are forbidden to commit any act in thought or deed that is impure and shameful.

What God requires of us is purity of heart and soul, all in keeping with our dignity as his children.

Q. 38 *What does the Sixth Commandment forbid?*
The Sixth Commandment forbids impurity of any kind: this means immoral actions, words, looks, books, pictures, and shows.

Q. 39 *What does the Sixth Commandment order?*
The Sixth Commandment orders us to be holy in body, conducting ourselves with the greatest respect for our own person and the person of others, as works of God and temples where he dwells with his presence and his grace.

Q. 40 *What does the Ninth Commandment forbid?*
The Ninth Commandment forbids impure thoughts and desires.

Q. 41 *What are we ordered to do by the Ninth Commandment?*
The Ninth Commandment orders us to practice perfect purity of soul and the greatest respect for family life.

St. Maria Goretti

In 1950, at Rome, a girl who had died at the age of twelve was declared a saint. She had been stabbed to death because she refused to commit an act of impurity. Her name is Maria Goretti.

Maria was born in Ancona, Italy, in 1890. Her father was a tenant farmer; his family moved a lot as he looked for work. He died when Maria was ten.

Maria never had the chance to go to school; she never learned to read or write. But she was carefully instructed in the Catholic faith by her mother, Assunta. She received her First Holy Communion when she was twelve.

Assunta had advised her daughter Maria as she had all her children: "Never, at any cost, never must you sin!" Maria never forgot.

Shortly after her First Communion, a nineteen-year-old boy who worked with Maria's family wanted her to be unchaste and threatened her with a knife. When she would not give in, he stabbed her to death.

Many years later, the man who had killed her repented and turned to a life of devotion. He joined those who sought her canonization.

Maria is the great saint of purity for our difficult age.

Words to Know:

chastity   impurity

Purity prepares the soul for love, and love confirms the soul in purity.

— Cardinal Newman

CHAPTER 14

Ownership

You will find very few things around you that someone does not own. The things around us may be owned by a group of people like a company, or by a larger community such as a city, state, or nation, or by a single person. Every person has the right to own property; groups have the same right. This requires respect for the right of ownership; all have the right to have their possessions safe from theft, damage, and destruction.

These rights are protected by the Seventh Commandment:

"You shall not steal."

This commandment regulates how we handle other peoples' possessions or property. It forbids the unjust taking of what belongs to another. If I take your record without asking you, I am guilty of theft. To be free from guilt I must return what I have stolen or replace it if I can, as well as confess my sin if the matter is serious. If I purposely damage your record by scratching it I have destroyed it, and justice demands that I make restitution—that is, pay for the damage.

We must have nothing to do with stolen property, even if we didn't steal it ourselves.

Neither can we claim to own something that belongs to someone else—as for example, when one student copies another's homework. Such a student is guilty of both stealing and lying, since he presents the work as his own.

On Loan

There are questions which come up about our duties and obligations when we make rightful use of another's property by permission. Perhaps we have borrowed a record to see how we like it before buying one of our own. Then we must return it in the same condition in which we received it. If we have damaged it, we must replace it. So too, in a store, we must handle merchandise with care and be honest if we damage something. We must always pay back

in full all loans and debts; if we don't we are stealing.

The Seventh Commandment also forbids any kind of deception or breach of contract in our dealings with others' property. This is called fraud. There is another evil practice called usury in which someone loans money at an excessively high rate of interest. This is a very bad thing, for someone who practices it is making money out of another person's great need.

We are also required to be just in payment for services or goods bought. We must always pay a worker what he has earned.

The Tenth Commandment,

> *"You shall not covet your neighbor's goods"*,

is meant to direct our desire for possessions.

There are two very common ways in which people break this commandment: envy and avarice. Both reveal that something is wrong with the way a person looks upon material goods. Envy is being resentful of another's success. The envious man is unhappy because he wants what another man has. Avarice is like greed. The avaricious man has an excessive desire for wealth. He always wants more, no matter how much he already has.

Justice and Charity

There are certain societies in which the right to own private property is denied. However, the right to private property is acknowledged by God in the Ten Commandments. He would not condemn stealing if nobody were to own anything.

Stealing is wrong because it is unjust. Thus, justice is the virtue that protects personal possessions. Justice obliges me to make restitution if I steal. It obliges my employer to pay me my due wage and obliges me to earn it with honest labor.

But the right to private property, protected by justice, is not a sufficient foundation for the happy life of a society; charity is needed.

For instance, the right to property may be acknowledged by everyone, while at the same time some persons have more than they need— even much more—and others do not have even a minimum required by human dignity.

Should my possessions, if they are many, be taken away from me to give to the poor? Would that be just? If not, should I forget the poor? Charity obliges me to share what I have with those who need decent food, clothing, and shelter. If people are in extreme need, then the taking of what is necessary to maintain life is not stealing since it is not the unjust taking of another's property. Jesus identifies himself with the poor when he says:

> Come. You have my Father's blessing! Inherit the Kingdom prepared for you from the creation of the world. For I was hungry and you gave me food, I was thirsty and you gave me drink. I was a stranger and you welcomed me, naked and you clothed me. I was ill and you comforted me, in prison and you came to visit me. . . . I assure you, as often as you did it for one of my least brothers, you did it for me. (Mt 25:34−36, 40)

Words to Know:

steal   envy   avarice   usury   fraud

> Be not anxious about what you have, but about what you are.
>
> — Pope St. Gregory

59

Spirit of Poverty

St. Francis of Assisi was known as "the poor man". He won this title by owning little more than the shirt on his back. If he was asked about his circumstances he would often reply that he was married to Lady Poverty. Francis meant that he loved poverty and never wanted to own anything.

This was a great shock to his father, who was a rich cloth merchant and had great plans for his son. But God had other plans. Francis's father, Pietro Bernardone, did not accept God's plans gracefully. The result was that father and son parted company. Pietro's plans were ruined, but a whole new world opened up for Francis. He roamed the hillsides of Assisi; he walked the byways praising God; he lived in the open; he prayed long hours; he begged; and he rebuilt a mountain chapel that had fallen into disrepair. Soon others began following him, until finally a great religious order grew up around Francis's example.

St. Francis is set before us as one who had the right attitude toward material possessions. We should not set our hearts on riches. Few of us are called to be as poor as Francis, but Our Lord addressed the following words to all men: "No man can serve two masters. He will either hate one and love the other or be attentive to one and despise the other. You cannot give yourself to God and money." (Mt 6:24)

Jesus means that a person who has his heart set on material possessions will not be able to pay attention to the Kingdom of God. Instead of looking for chances to serve God, to pray, or to study Our Lord's words and example, such a person will be looking for chances to collect more riches. (This may mean piling up much more than one needs.) One cannot have one's mind on both things—God and money. It must be one or the other.

Serving God wholeheartedly, of course, need not mean choosing Lady Poverty, like Francis; but it cannot mean choosing riches instead of God's plan, like his father. We should try to be content with what we have and take reasonable care of our interests.

"Keep your life free from the love of money, and be content with what you have."

(Hebrews 13:5)

Q. 42 *What is forbidden by the Seventh Commandment?*
The Seventh Commandment forbids damaging our neighbor's property. This includes thefts, destructive actions, usury, fraud in contracts and in services, and assistance in any such acts.

Q. 43 *What does the Seventh Commandment order us to do?*
The Seventh Commandment orders us to give back the property belonging to others, to repair damages that we are responsible for, to honor debts, and to pay a just wage to working men.

Q. 44 *What does the Tenth Commandment forbid?*
The Tenth Commandment forbids the unrestrained desire for riches, without regard for the rights and welfare of our neighbor.

Q. 45 *What does the Tenth Commandment order us to do?*
The Tenth Commandment orders us to be just and moderate in the desire to improve our own condition of life, and to suffer with patience the hardships and other sufferings permitted by the Lord for our good, because "we must undergo many trials if we are to enter into the reign of God". (Acts 14:22)

CHAPTER 15

Backed by Truth

The Eighth Commandment,

"You shall not bear false witness against your neighbor",

requires that we speak the truth always, but especially in matters involving the good name and honor of others. Truth is very important to us. If men were not truthful it would be impossible for us to live together.

When he was on trial before Pilate, Jesus said: "The reason I was born, the reason why I came into the world, is to testify to the truth. Anyone committed to the truth hears my voice." "Truth!" said Pilate. "What does that mean?" (Jn 18:37–38) Evidently Pilate, who may at one time have been concerned about truth, about the meaning of life, about right and wrong, no longer cared, or had given up on it and decided there was no such thing.

But Our Lord had come as a witness to the truth. And Pilate could not help being impressed. This is perhaps what led him to make a few weak attempts to save Our Lord's life; but, as we know, Pilate gave in under pressure and agreed to a lie by condemning Jesus.

We all know what harm can be done just by one lie. The Eighth Commandment tells us we must never tell even a single lie. But it also directs all our powers of communication. We are obliged to speak the truth and must never intend to deceive another when he has the right to the truth.

Lying

A lie is a deliberate attempt to mislead others. It is always sinful. We may not lie to get out of trouble, to cover up for a friend, or to get into a movie. Even if what we want is good, we may not lie to get it.

We can be strongly tempted to lie sometimes—it can seem so simple and so harmless. But we must always tell the truth to those who have a right to know.

Hypocrisy

A special kind of untruthfulness is hypocrisy, when someone pretends to be better than he really is or pretends to believe something he really denies just to impress people. Jesus condemned this sin many times. However, it is not wrong to be on one's best behavior with those on whom one wishes to make a good impression.

Promises and Oaths

An important aspect of honesty is keeping one's word. One makes one's word true by living up to it. It is telling the truth about one's future actions.

In taking an oath in a courtroom one promises to tell the truth with God as one's witness. This is very serious. It is always a serious sin to lie in an important matter, but to lie under oath before God is much worse. Such a lie is called perjury.

Another's Good Name

However, there are times when we may be telling the truth and still sin. We must always speak the truth if we speak at all, but sometimes it is more prudent or charitable for us to remain silent. There are even times when we must not tell what we know to be true, for to do so would be wrong.

We have a precious possession that we may take for granted: our good name or reputation. We may hardly think of it, unless it is endangered. But if it is hurt or lost we see how precious it is to us. "A good name is more desirable than great riches." (Prov 22:1) Regaining a good name once it is lost is very difficult; just think how hard it must be for an ex-convict to find a job. To damage a person's reputation is a serious matter. Therefore, one must have a very good reason for revealing anything about a person which would hurt his good name.

As for ourselves, we should take care to be worthy of a good reputation—not by seeking fame and renown, but by loving God and our neighbor and by being known as faithful followers of Christ.

There may be times when we are called upon to reveal what we know about someone— for instance, in legal proceedings—but we must be very careful about what we do with damaging facts, even if they are true.

How much worse, then, is a damaging story which is not true! Irresponsible or malicious use of the truth to harm another is called *detraction* and is a serious sin. The use of lies

to hurt someone is called *calumny* or *slander* and is an even greater sin. There is a grave obligation to repair the damage done by any of these sins.

Rash Judgment

Besides being careful in what we say about someone, we must also be careful in what we think. There is a sin called *rash judgment* which is to judge another person's character on flimsy evidence. This does not mean that we may never make a judgment, but that we must be very careful about it. Otherwise someone may lose our esteem without a good reason. We should be very slow to judge.

Gossip

As a rule, we should not talk about the faults of others unless there is a good and important reason to do so. Gossiping usually consists of talking about the faults of others or exaggerating them. People who gossip may deal with facts, but they destroy another person's good name to satisfy idle curiosity. We must not be willing even to listen to people who gossip about others.

Secrets

We must keep any promise we have made, including the promise to keep a secret. If someone tells us a secret, or if we find out something that must be kept secret for another person's good, then we must be silent about what we have learned.

Our power of speech is a precious gift, a gift that must not be used to hurt others! Jesus says:

> I tell you, on the day of judgment men will render account for every careless word they utter; for by your words you will be justified, and by your words you will be condemned. (Mt 12:36−37)

Words to Know:

slander	flattery	detraction
rash judgment	gossip	false witness

"Never let evil talk pass your lips; say only the good things men need to hear, things that will really help them."

(Ephesians 4:29)

Q. 46 *What is forbidden by the Eighth Commandment?*
The Eighth Commandment forbids all falsehood and unjust damage to another person's reputation. This includes false witness, slander, lies, detraction, flattery, unfounded suspicion, and rash judgment.

Q. 47 *What does the Eighth Commandment order?*
The Eighth Commandment orders us to speak the truth responsibly and to avoid rash judgment of our neighbor's actions.

Q. 48 *What is a person required to do who has damaged his neighbor's good reputation by accusing him falsely or speaking badly of him?*
He who has damaged his neighbor's good reputation by false accusation or bad talk about him must repair the damage he has done, so far as he is able.

CHAPTER 16

The Beatitudes

When he was about thirty years old, Jesus began his public life by being baptized in a preparatory rite by St. John in the Jordan River. When he was baptized, the Holy Spirit came down in the form of a dove and rested above Jesus, and a voice from the heavens said: "This is my beloved Son. My favor rests on him." (Mt 3:16−17)

Following his baptism, Jesus was led by the Spirit into the wilderness, where he prayed and fasted for forty days and overcame the devil's temptations.

After this, Jesus set out to preach the Good News of God's Kingdom. He was a teacher, a reformer, and a miracle worker, and he was the perfect living example of everything he taught. He even raised the dead to life. He taught everywhere: in the fields, on the roads, on the hillsides, in the synagogues, by lakes, and even from a boat. He often taught in parables, using for examples things people used and saw every day, from the lilies of the field to the sparrows of the air.

Jesus didn't come to abolish the Old Law but to fulfill it with the New. He built on the Ten Commandments and the "you shall not" prohibitions by giving positive exhortations to live the Christian life. Among these exhortations are those called the eight Beatitudes. They sum up the blessings and joys in store for people who follow Jesus and his way of life. A beatitude is a blessing or special happiness of a spiritual nature.

Jesus emphasized that these blessings are open to everyone, no matter how poor or uneducated or sick or unwanted a person may be. This contradicted the Scribes and Pharisees, who taught that poverty or bad health was a punishment and a sign of God's disfavor.

The Beatitudes

1. "Blessed are the poor in spirit, for theirs is the Kingdom of Heaven."

The poor in spirit are those who may have material possessions but who are ready to give them up when self-sacrifice is called for. They value heavenly treasure above everything else and never lose sight of it.

You may remember the rich young man who turned away from following Jesus because this man was attached to his many possessions. The poor in spirit do just the opposite: when Jesus calls, they leave all things to follow him. Because their hearts are not filled with things of earth, God fills their hearts with himself.

2. "Blessed are those who mourn, for they shall be comforted."

Mourning, in this Beatitude, means sorrow for sin and sorrow over the loss, by separation or by death, of someone dear to us.

Jesus promises the sorrowful that they will get the strength they need to stand firm in their trials and troubles and even to grow through their sorrows in their friendship with God.

3. "Blessed are the meek, for they shall inherit the earth."

The meek are those who are truly humble and kind. They don't think of themselves as being better than other people. They accept and recognize the gifts God has given them with gratitude and patience and without complaint.

4. "Blessed are those who hunger and thirst for righteousness, for they shall be satisfied."

Blessed is the heart that wants what God wants! If we desire to be righteous and holy, Jesus will help us and our desire will be fulfilled. Jesus promises joy to those who do God's will.

5. "Blessed are the merciful, for they shall obtain mercy."

Mercy is love shown to the unlovable and to those who have been unjust and ungrateful. The merciful forgive others their offenses. They, in turn, will receive mercy from God. Jesus said: "If you forgive the faults of others, your heavenly Father will forgive you yours." (Mt 6:14)

6. "Blessed are the pure in heart, for they shall see God."

The pure in heart are those who live chaste lives and are free of all excessive love of earthly things. They have put God first in their lives. Because they are single-hearted, they can feel God's presence in this life and will see him face to face in the next.

7. *"Blessed are the peacemakers, for they shall be called the sons of God."*

Psalm 132 begins: "Behold, how good and how pleasant it is for brothers to dwell together in unity."

Peacemakers go out of their way to remove the obstacles that keep men apart. They work especially hard to bring sinners back to God.

Jesus promises that peacemakers will be God's special children here on earth and will enjoy heavenly glory in the family of the saints.

8. *"Blessed are those who are persecuted for righteousness' sake, for theirs is the Kingdom of Heaven."*

Jesus suffered everything to witness to the truth. If we are persecuted because we are loyal to Jesus and his Church, we will know a little of what he suffered on the Cross to free us from sin and death. But we will also share in the joy of his Resurrection, his gift of eternal life with God.

***

The eight Beatitudes are the counsels of the New Testament; instead of being prohibitions, they are positive exhortations to live in intimacy with Jesus Christ. Each has attached to it a promise of great rewards.

Perhaps you have been thinking how difficult this is—how impossible, even, for human strength alone to live up to. You're right—it *is* hard!

That is why Christ has left us a great source of divine power in the Holy Eucharist. If we take the Commandments and the Beatitudes seriously and desire to live up to them, we will feel the call to unite ourselves to Christ by receiving the Holy Eucharist often—perhaps even daily. And we will be well on our way to living the authentic Christian life.

Words to Know:

the eight Beatitudes

PART TWO

The Holy Mass

CHAPTER 17

At the Last Supper

Let us begin by reading chapter six of St. John's Gospel.

Jesus shocked many of his followers by saying that he would give them his Body to eat and his Blood to drink, and that they would not have life in them unless they accepted it. At this many of his followers left him. Peter answered for those who remained faithful. When Jesus asked them, "Will you, too, leave me?" Peter said, "To whom shall we go, Lord? You have the words of eternal life." (Jn 6:68–69)

Peter and the faithful disciples did not foresee how Jesus was going to do what he said; they didn't have the slightest idea how it could be possible. But they had come to know and love Jesus; they had come to hunger for the words of eternal life that came from him; and they believed.

Just before he told them this, Jesus demonstrated his power by feeding a crowd of about five thousand people with a few loaves and fishes, and he had announced greater things to come. But he did not explain. When the time came for him to leave his apostles, Jesus gave them a treasure of immeasurable richness— his own Self in the Eucharist. With the utmost simplicity he found a way to give them his Body and Blood to eat and drink: he changed bread into his Body and wine into his Blood.

This wonderful event took place at Jesus' Last Supper with his apostles the night before he died. They were celebrating one of the great festivals of the Jewish people, the Passover. With Jesus' action the sacrifice of the Old Covenant was ended and the sacrifice of the New Covenant established.

The Passover

The Passover commemorated God's rescue of his chosen people from slavery in Egypt, when he worked great signs and wonders through his servant Moses to strike the fear of God into the hearts of the Egyptians so that Pharaoh would free the Hebrews and allow them to depart.

Actually, Pharaoh was very stubborn about it until one night the angel of death passed through Egypt, striking down the firstborn sons of the Egyptians.

The Hebrews had been instructed by God through Moses to offer a special sacrifice that night: a spotless lamb, one for each family. Every Hebrew dwelling was to be marked on the doorpost with the blood of the lamb so that the angel of death would pass over without harming those within.

After this event the Egyptians finally let the Hebrews go, for the fear of God had fallen on them.

All of this is important if we are to understand what Jesus did at the Last Supper. We can see the slavery of the Hebrew people as an image of the slavery of all people in sin. And just as God freed the Hebrews, he frees us. The sacrifice that frees man from sin is the crucifixion and death of Our Lord Jesus Christ. He is the Passover Lamb.

Each year the Hebrew people observed the anniversary of the Passover—and the mighty events that led to their freedom—with a special meal. Each family would offer a Paschal lamb in sacrifice and would eat it with unleavened bread and bitter herbs. These were details that recalled the original Passover.

Jesus and his apostles were celebrating this special meal when Jesus ''took bread, blessed it, broke it, and gave it to his disciples. 'Take this and eat it,' he said; 'this is my Body.' Then he took a cup, gave thanks, and gave it to them. 'All of you must drink from it,' he said, 'for this is my Blood, the blood of the Covenant, to be poured out on behalf of many for the forgiveness of sins.' '' (Mt 26:26−28)

The Perfect Victim

From the time of Adam's fall, men have felt the need to make a public offering to God to make up for their sins and ask for mercy. The firstfruits of a harvest, a lamb or a goat—something needed for life—these things would be destroyed on an altar by a priest to indicate that, like everything that exists, they belong to God. Men desired to be restored to that friendship with God which sin had broken. Their sacrifices were an attempt to do this.

Offering a sacrifice has four distinct purposes: to adore God, to thank him, to make up for sin, and to ask his help.

Before the coming of Christ a great many sacrifices were offered to God, but not one of them offered a victim that could atone for men's sins. Alone, men were unable to offer to God anything so fitting and precious that it could make up for such a grave offense against God. But God loves us so much and so much desired our reconciliation to him that he gave us an acceptable victim that would satisfy our debt.

Jesus, given to us by the Father, was that acceptable victim. This divine victim was sacrificed upon the Cross to make peace between Heaven and earth once and for all.

The word *oblation* is used to indicate the total offering of a victim or gift in a sacrifice. In the oblation of Jesus Christ, he was both priest and victim. For he was held on the Cross by his love alone; at any moment he could have come down from the Cross, but he would not. He truly offered himself. To all appearances he died like a criminal, but, unlike anyone else who was ever crucified, he freely laid down his life.

Being God and Man

When Jesus took the bread at the Last Supper and said, ''This is my Body'', he made himself present on the table as the gift of the sacrifice. He stood over the gift and looked down upon it, but the gift was no longer bread; it was his Body, it was himself. He did the same thing with the wine; it became his precious Blood. Jesus could do this because he was God as well as man.

At the Last Supper, the apostles received the first Holy Communion, and each apostle received Jesus complete and entire—not part of Jesus but the whole Jesus—Body, Blood, Soul, and Divinity, God and man. The whole Jesus went to Andrew, to Peter, to John, to Philip, to each one. And so he comes to us, too, when we receive Holy Communion. The apostles were united with Christ and filled with grace. So are we.

But what did the apostles see when Jesus said, "This is my Body. . . . This is my Blood"? What they saw still looked like bread and wine. What had been bread still had the same weight, color, and taste; what had been wine still had the same taste, odor, and color. But its *substance*, the underlying reality which makes it what it is, had been changed. The looks and other properties known by the senses are called the *appearances*; the Body and Blood of Jesus kept the *appearances* of bread and wine. This mysterious change that took place in the bread and wine is called "transubstantiation", which means change of substance.

The Everlasting Sacrifice

After the apostles had each received Holy Communion, Jesus said to them, "Do this in remembrance of me." (Lk 22:19) When he said this he made them priests; for by telling them to do what he had just done—to change bread and wine into his Body and Blood—he gave them the power to do it.

The greatest power of the priesthood is the power to offer this sacrifice of Jesus' Body and Blood. It is the same sacrifice that Jesus offered at the Last Supper and the next day on the Cross. Through this power the Body and Blood of Jesus continue to be offered to God under the appearances of bread and wine whenever the Mass is celebrated.

So God left us an everlasting sacrifice of such richness and power that nothing else can be compared to it.

The apostles used their powers to feed the new Church of Christ with the Bread from Heaven; and they shared their power with other men, co-workers and their successors, so that the Church could continue from generation to generation to offer the great sacrifice, making it present to all who seek it, until the end of time.

Words to Know:

Passover   Last Supper
transubstantiation   mystery
Eucharist   oblation   Victim

"I will lift up the cup of salvation and will offer a sacrifice of praise."

(Psalm 115)

Q. 49 *When did Jesus Christ institute the Eucharist?*
Jesus Christ instituted the Eucharist at the Last Supper, before his Passion, when he consecrated and changed bread and wine into his Body and Blood and distributed it to the apostles, commanding them to do the same thing in his memory.

Q. 50 *Why did Jesus Christ institute the Eucharist?*
Jesus Christ instituted the Eucharist so that in the Mass there would be a permanent sacrifice of the New Testament and in Holy Communion a spiritual food for our souls, and a memorial of his love and of his Passion.

Q. 51 *What is a sacrifice?*
A sacrifice is the public offering to God of a thing which is destroyed to profess that God is Creator and Supreme Ruler to whom everything belongs.

CHAPTER 18

The Living Sacrifice

Jesus Christ, through whom all good things come to us, died on Calvary and rose again from the dead. His sacrifice redeemed the human race. Every day that sacrifice is renewed in the Holy Mass. That is what the Mass is all about. The Mass is the same sacrifice as the sacrifice at Calvary; it not only recalls that sacrifice but continues it.

Jesus gave us the precious gift of the Eucharist for two reasons: so that we might have eternal life and so that we might have an acceptable sacrifice to offer continually to the Father.

As Frank Sheed expressed it, "The Mass *is* Calvary, as Christ now offers it to his Father." The Victim offered is the same—Jesus himself. He is present as he made himself present under the appearances of bread and wine at the Last Supper. The Priest is one and the same; for the priest at our altar acts in the person of Jesus to change the bread and wine into the Body and Blood of the Lord.

The difference between the sacrifice of the Cross and that of the Mass is the way in which it is carried out. On the Cross Jesus offered himself, shedding his Blood for our redemption. On the altar Jesus is offered through the ministry of the priest without shedding his Blood again.

A Memorial

Besides being a sacrifice, the Mass is a memorial by which until the end of time we call to mind the death of Christ. Christ said to his apostles, "Do this in memory of me."

He did not mean, however, that the Mass would be *only* a memorial. In the Mass we not only remember Christ's death on the Cross, but Christ brings his sacrifice before us in a real though sacramental way.

Mass is a memorial of Christ's Resurrection as well. The Church teaches that it is "a memorial of his death and Resurrection". Here, too, the reality is more than a recollection. For the Chief Priest at Mass is the Risen Christ who is present in the Eucharist.

The Four Ends of Mass

Holy Mass is the perfect prayer. So it has the same ends, or purposes, as prayer.

1. The Mass is an act of supreme worship; it

"He sits forever at the right hand of God, offering for our sins a sacrifice that can never be repeated."

(Hebrews 10:12)

is Christ's greatest gift to his Church. Men with nothing worthy to offer God have now been given a Victim and a sacrifice of infinite value.

2. The Mass is a prayer of thanksgiving; the word "eucharist" actually means "thanksgiving". We have so much to thank God for: our lives, with all that they contain of family and friends, people, places, and things. Most of all, there is the supernatural life of grace given to us by Jesus Christ, Our Savior. It is through the life of grace that we have hope of reaching Heaven and can enjoy great happiness even now.

Through the Mass we have the chance to thank God for all his benefits, most of all for his generosity and mercy in sending us Jesus, his Son. And it is Jesus, his gift to us, whom we now offer back to him. God is infinitely pleased with this gift that he has put in our hands.

3. The Mass is a means of making satisfaction for sins. We pray: "Lamb of God, you take away the sins of the world, have mercy on us . . . grant us peace."

Are we asking Jesus to do something that he has already done? Are we asking him to take away the sins of the world again and again, every time the Mass is offered?

No; there is really only one Mass, and it was

offered on Calvary. And it is this one Mass that is offered on all our altars. Through the gift of the Mass, Jesus has extended his sacrifice in time and space. Our participation at Mass is our time to be with Christ at the Cross.

4. The Mass is our best means of petitioning the Father and obtaining the graces we ask for both for ourselves and for others. In the Mass we are offering to God the perfect sacrifice, the most pleasing offering we have to give, and God will be pleased by our offering so great a gift.

Words to Know:

sacrament   memorial
make satisfaction for

Q. 52   *What is the Holy Mass?*
The Holy Mass is the sacrifice of the Body and Blood of Jesus Christ, which is offered on the altar by the priest to God, under the appearances of bread and wine, in memory of the sacrifice of the Cross and in renewal of the sacrifice of the Cross.

Q. 53   *Is the sacrifice of the Mass the same sacrifice as the Cross?*
The sacrifice of the Mass is the very sacrifice of the Cross; the only difference is in the manner of performing it.

Q. 54   *Is there any difference between the sacrifice of the Cross and the sacrifice of the Mass?*
The manner in which the sacrifice is offered is different. On the Cross Christ shed his Blood and was physically slain, while in the Mass there is no physical shedding of blood or death, because Christ can die no more; on the Cross Christ gained merit and made satisfaction for us; while in the Mass he applies to us the merits and satisfaction of his death on the Cross.

Q. 55   *Why is the Mass offered to God?*
The Mass is offered to God to give him the supreme worship of adoration; to thank him for his blessings to us; to make satisfaction for our sins; and to obtain graces for the good of the faithful, living and dead.

CHAPTER 19

The Feast of God

At Mass we celebrate the death and Resurrection of the Lord in a sacred banquet. These are truly matters for celebration—for taking time out for special activities to underline the significance of our redemption and to rejoice with Our Risen Lord.

However, this is no ordinary, casual celebration like a birthday party or a big family meal. This is a sacred celebration; it is *holy*. It is time consecrated to God, dedicated to him, set aside for him alone. Therefore we should approach this celebration with an attitude of reverence and profound respect. We express reverence by our attitude and our actions: by proper dress, by silence, by genuflection, by prayerfulness. When we understand this, we are ready to consider Holy Mass as a celebration. The mysteries we celebrate are worthy of the deepest awe. With Jesus, as with anyone whom we love, friendship and respect must go together. But Jesus is more than just a friend; he is God. We must never forget who he is and who we are; he is the Creator, and we are his creatures.

Sacred Banquet

What is the special activity which makes the Mass a celebration? It is the sacred banquet, the holy meal—Communion. A common meal has always been a way of celebrating important occasions.

A big family meal is a good example of a celebration. We show that the cause for celebration is important to us, not only as individuals but as a family, a group, a community. It is important enough, in fact, to take a group of individuals, each of whom could have gone his own way, and bring them together in a unifying action. Why do we all do something together? Because it is important to us. Those who participate become part of something greater than any one person.

Table of the Lord

We have seen that the Mass is the representation of Christ's sacrifice on Calvary. We have watched and prayed with the priest. We now have the wonderful opportunity to go to Holy Communion, to receive Christ in the Eucharist.

In Old Testament sacrifices, the people offered God a gift, such as a lamb. The lamb was slaughtered to offer it up. But this was not all. To complete the religious ritual or celebration of the sacrifice, the people would eat the lamb. The gift that they offered was received back as a gift. The people were trying to be in closer union with God by partaking of something that had been offered to and accepted by God.

As we have seen, the Mass is a sacrifice far greater than any other. It is the one and only perfect sacrifice. But here, too, the religious ritual is not really complete until we partake of the gift that has been offered.

We join the priest in offering Jesus to the Father; the Father accepts our gift and gives it back to us to eat. Therefore, the Mass is considered a feast, a meal, a sacred banquet. It can be thought of as a big family meal as long as two points are kept in mind: the family consists of all those joined in the brotherhood of Christ, and the food is the sacred Body and Blood of Christ. Holy Communion is meant to be received in the communal religious service which is the Mass. We are to go forward as God's family—not alone but in company.

In the Our Father, we pray for our "daily bread", expressing our trust in God who provides for all our earthly needs. On another level, our "daily bread" is Christ, the spiritual bread in the eucharistic banquet that we need in order to be made holy.

And we pray to "our" Father, not just "my" Father, because we are meant to grow into the perfect unity of a happy and glorious community—a family—in the mystical Body of Christ.

O Sacred Banquet,
in which Christ is received,
the memory of his Passion is renewed,
the mind is filled with grace,
and a pledge of future glory is given us.
Alleluia.

CHAPTER 20

Promise and Fulfillment

Remember the text of St. John's Gospel we read back in Chapter 17?

"This is a hard saying."

These were the words with which many of his followers greeted Jesus' announcement of the Holy Eucharist. If Jesus had been misunderstood he could have set things straight before they walked away from him. But Jesus did not stop them. In fact, the Gospel says: "Jesus was fully aware that his disciples were murmuring in protest at what he had said. 'Does it shake your faith?' he asked them." (Jn 6:61) The Gospel goes on to say: "From this time on, many of his disciples broke away and would not remain in his company any longer." (Jn 6:66)

What had Jesus said, exactly, which they would not accept?

He who feeds on my Flesh and drinks my Blood has life eternal, and I will raise him up on the last day. For my Flesh is real food and my Blood real drink. (Jn 6:54−55)

And what did those who did not believe say?

"How can he give us his Flesh to eat?" (Jn 6:52)

We Have Come To Believe

The Gospel goes on to tell us:

Jesus then said to the Twelve, "Do you want to leave me too?" Simon Peter answered him, "Lord, to whom shall we go? You have the words of eternal life; we have come to believe; we are convinced that you are God's holy one." (Jn 6:67−69)

Jesus had not led his followers to this point to catch them unprepared. As Peter put it, they had "come to believe".

The apostles believed not because they understood, but because they had faith in Jesus. This is what Jesus was looking for. The Gospel says: "All this they said to him, 'What must we do to perform the works of God?' Jesus replied: 'This is the work of God: have faith in the One whom he sent.' " (Jn 6:28−29) Jesus had given them more than sufficient evidence to believe in him. He had been going about doing good, teaching and preaching the good news of the Kingdom of God, and performing many miracles.

In every generation Jesus looks for generous people who really hear him, who really want to be his followers and really put their faith in him, who will not turn away because of the "hard saying" about the Eucharist, who will say with St. Peter: "We have come to believe; we are convinced that you are God's holy one." (Jn 6:69)

My Flesh is Food Indeed

Just what was Christ offering the crowds when he announced the Eucharist? He said that his "Flesh is food indeed" and his "Blood is real drink". We have seen that he meant to be taken literally. However, he did not mean that the Eucharist would be food for our bodies. The Eucharist is spiritual food, nourishment for our souls.

What happens when we receive the Eucharist worthily? Because the Eucharist truly is the Body and Blood of Jesus, it is the source of all grace. It can transform us by the increase of sanctifying grace, which is God's life in the soul. We grow in holiness, which means that we become more like Jesus. Receiving the Eucharist can pardon our venial sins. Because it is such "rich and nourishing" food for our souls, it cancels out our lesser failings. It also

strengthens us to overcome temptations and helps us to break bad habits.

Christ has a plan for extending his Kingdom to the whole world: he offers his followers the invitation to become other Christs. Those who feed on his Body and Blood have life in him—Christ's life, which does not destroy our personality, but perfects it and enriches it and preserves it to life everlasting.

"I am the Living Bread which came down from Heaven; if anyone eats of this Bread he will live forever."

(John 6:50)

Q. 56 *What is the Eucharist?*

The Eucharist is the sacrament which contains the Body, Blood, Soul, and Divinity of our Lord Jesus Christ, under the appearances of bread and wine, for the nourishment of souls.

Q. 57 *Is the same Jesus Christ present in the Eucharist who was born on earth of the Virgin Mary?*

Yes, the same Jesus Christ is truly present in the Eucharist who is in Heaven, and who was born on earth of the Virgin Mary.

Q. 58 *Why do you believe that Jesus Christ is truly present in the Eucharist?*

I believe that Jesus Christ is truly present in the Eucharist because he himself said that the consecrated bread and wine are his Body and Blood, and because the Church teaches this; but it is a mystery, a great mystery.

Q. 59 *What effect does the Eucharist have on one who receives it worthily?*

In him who receives it worthily, the Holy Eucharist preserves and increases grace, which is the life of the soul, just as food does for the life of the body. The Holy Eucharist takes away venial sin and preserves us from mortal sins, and it gives spiritual joy and consolation by increasing charity and the hope of eternal life of which it is the pledge.

CHAPTER 21

New Life

When Jesus died, his disciples, helped by Joseph of Arimathea, came and took his body and buried it in a tomb cut in rock in a garden. This was done in haste, because they had to prepare for the Sabbath.

But then, what? Was it all over, the glorious dream, the visible evidence of the power of God? The Messiah was dead, their beloved Jesus. The apostles were in hiding for fear of the Jewish leaders.

Then, on the first day of the week, some of the women who had travelled with Jesus and the apostles set out for the tomb with spices to anoint the body of Jesus and to tend to the details of ceremonial burial which had not been observed the day he died. On the way they began to wonder who would open the tomb for them, since a great stone had been rolled into place to seal it.

But when they got there the stone had been rolled back and an angel from Heaven was sitting on it. He informed them that Jesus, who had been crucified, had risen from the dead. He invited them into the tomb to see for themselves.

The women looked in and saw that the tomb was empty. Then the angel said: "Now he is going before you to Galilee; it is there you will see him." (Mt 28:7)

The women hurried back to the apostles, filled with awe and great joy. But the apostles did not believe their marvelous news. Peter and John set out to see for themselves; they found the empty tomb, with nothing in it but the wrappings in which Jesus had been buried.

When the Apostles were gathered together Jesus suddenly appeared among them. "Peace be with you", he said.

The apostles were in a panic, thinking they were seeing a ghost. Jesus reassured them, telling them that it was really him. He invited them to touch his solid flesh and asked for something to eat. They gave him a piece of cooked fish and he ate it to show that he was not a ghost.

In these and other ways Jesus helped them realize that he had risen from the dead and that he was really standing there before them. How they rejoiced!

Then Jesus breathed on them, strengthening them with the Holy Spirit and giving them the power to forgive sins: "Receive the Holy Spirit. If you forgive men's sins, they are forgiven them; if you hold them bound they are held bound." (Jn 20:23) He told them that they were to be witnesses to him to all nations, beginning at Jerusalem.

After that, Jesus did not remain with them, but he appeared to them on several occasions, putting the finishing touches to his work on earth. During one of his appearances by the Sea of Galilee, he asked Peter, "Do you love me more than these others?'' Peter answered yes. Twice more Jesus asked, ''Peter, do you love me?'' Feeling hurt, Peter answered, ''Lord, you know everything. You know that I love you.'' (Jn 21:15−17)

Jesus was giving Peter a chance to declare his love three times before witnesses because Peter had denied Jesus three times before witnesses when Jesus was on trial.

When Peter had answered his questions, Jesus instructed him, ''Feed my lambs; feed my sheep.'' There Jesus made Peter the universal shepherd of all his followers, the first pope. At last Jesus simply said to Peter: ''Follow me.''

Forty days after his Resurrection, Jesus ascended to Heaven in the presence of his followers. Before this he had instructed the apostles not to go anywhere until he sent them the Holy Spirit, who would lead them in all truth and give them special power to extend Christ's Church to every part of the earth. He promised to remain with his Church always, even to the end of the world.

What happened next is recorded in the book of the Bible called the Acts of the Apostles. It tells of the coming of the Holy Spirit in the form of tongues of fire, of the conversion of St. Paul and the works of the apostles, and of the wonderful early days of the Church and the first Christian communities.

Resurrected Life

When Jesus rose from the dead on Easter Sunday he proved that he was truly the Son of God, as he had said. This meant that his death had not been in vain. He really had redeemed the world from sin. It also meant that the powers that he had given his apostles were real, and so were his promises to send the Holy Spirit and to remain always with his Church.

But Jesus did more than just pay for our sins by his death on Calvary. His Resurrection on Easter Sunday was a sign that he had also brought us new life. This new life is the life of sanctifying grace, God's own life within us, which enables us to desire and to do what God wants and what will truly make us happy.

Jesus' Resurrection is also a sign of hope that we too will one day rise from the dead just as he did.

''I am the Resurrection and the Life.''   *(John 11:25)*

Q. 60 *After his death, what did Jesus Christ do?*

After his death, Jesus Christ descended to a place of rest of the souls of the just who had died up to that time to take them with him into Heaven. Then he rose from the dead, taking up his body which had been buried.

Q. 61 *What did Jesus Christ do after his Resurrection?*

After his Resurrection, Jesus Christ remained on earth forty days. Then he ascended to Heaven, where he sits at the right hand of God the Father almighty.

Q. 62 *Why did Jesus Christ remain on earth forty days after his Resurrection?*

Jesus Christ remained on earth forty days after his Resurrection in order to show that he had really and truly risen from the dead, to confirm his disciples in their faith in him, and to instruct them more profoundly in his teaching.

CHAPTER 22

Come into the Lord's Presence Singing for Joy

We have been studying the death and Resurrection of Our Lord Jesus Christ by which he redeemed all mankind. We have seen that the Mass is the re-presentation of this saving sacrifice. Now we will look at each part of the Mass.

We should approach not only Mass but the church building itself with the proper attitude. This means getting ready to take part in public worship of God. We get ready outwardly by wearing suitable clothes. We get ready inwardly by understanding our purpose in coming: to offer the Holy Sacrifice of the Mass with the priest and to be nourished by the Word of God and the precious Body and Blood of Our Lord Jesus Christ. We will come eagerly if we have thought deeply about the meaning of all these things.

The main parts of the Mass are the Liturgy of the Word and the Liturgy of the Eucharist. (The word *liturgy* means the official public worship of the Church.) But before these two parts comes a smaller part called the **Introductory Rites**. The Introductory Rites prepare us to take part worthily and to focus our hearts and our minds on the Mass.

First there is the *Entrance Antiphon* or *Hymn* during which the priest and the ministers enter the church and go to the altar. It is accompanied by signs of reverence, such as the carrying of candles, incense, and the Lectionary, the book which contains the Scripture readings used at Mass.

After the entrance song, the priest and the people make the Sign of the Cross. The priest greets the people: "The Lord be with you"; and the people answer:"And also with you".

Next is the *Penitential Rite*. The priest invites the people to think of their sins and be sorry for them. Then we all acknowledge our sins together, using one of three possible prayers of confession. This is not the same

thing as the sacrament of Confession, but it helps to purify our hearts.

The prayer of confession usually used is called the *Confiteor*. It begins: "I confess to Almighty God, and to you, my brothers and sisters . . .", and it is followed by the invocations, "Lord, have mercy; Christ, have mercy; Lord, have mercy", or, "Kyrie eleison; Christe eleison; Kyrie eleison."

The Penitential Rite reminds us that merely coming to Mass doesn't make us any better than the rest of mankind. It reminds us that we are all in desperate need of God's forgiveness. Put another way, we must remember that Almighty God is Almighty God and that "we are a set of perfectly ridiculous creatures", as Msgr. Ronald Knox put it. Then we begin to see things in the right perspective.

After asking for forgiveness we are ready to praise God and to recall that his divine Son became man to redeem us from our sins and make us children of his Heavenly Father. We do so in the *Gloria*, a prayer that was once a Christmas hymn and begins with the words with which the angels greeted the shepherds: "Glory to God in the highest, and peace to his people on earth."

In this prayer we offer God praise, honor, and adoration, addressing Father, Son, and Holy Spirit. In particular, we plead with the God-man Jesus Christ to hear our prayers and ask him to give us a share in his sacrifice and his victory over death as they are re-presented in the Mass.

The Introductory Rites are concluded with the *Opening Prayer* or *Collect*. The priest invites the people to pray, and together they may spend some moments in silence so that they can realize that they are in God's presence and make their petitions. Then the priest says the prayer that expresses the theme of the particular Mass, whether it be, for example, a

Sunday, the feast day of a saint, or a feast of the Blessed Virgin.

These prayers are determined by the day of the Liturgical Year. The Liturgical Year is the Church's calendar; it has its own seasons and special feast days. We know about Advent and Lent, the two penitential seasons, and there are other seasons in the Liturgical Year. The seasons are to remind us of the life and teachings of Jesus and to help us live as he wants us to.

Not only are certain prayers and the readings of the Mass determined by the liturgical season; so are the church decorations and the priest's vestments. The color of the vestment is an indication of what season or feast day is being celebrated.

Words to Know:

liturgy

89

"I will go up to the altar of God, the Giver of youth and happiness."

(Psalm 43)

Introductory Rites

Entrance Antiphon (Hymn)
Greeting of the People
Penitential Rite
Gloria
Opening Prayer (Collect)

CHAPTER 23

Speak Lord, Your Servant is Listening

As we have seen, the Introductory Rites involve our speaking to God. We pray for God's forgiveness in the Penitential Rite, praise his goodness in the Gloria, and pray the Collect. The next part of the Mass, the **Liturgy of the Word**, is just the opposite: now God speaks to us!

At Sunday Mass there are three readings from the Bible. The *First Reading* is usually from the Old Testament. (During the Easter season it is from the Acts of the Apostles.) From the Old Testament we learn the history of creation and of God's chosen people, the Hebrews. Sometimes we hear prophecies of the coming of the Savior. And many Old Testament events foreshadow the Gospel. For example, the Passover lamb foretells, or prefigures, the Holy Eucharist.

The First Reading is followed by the *Responsorial Psalm*, the reading or singing of a Psalm with a refrain that we repeat. The Psalms express every kind of prayer: praise, thanksgiving, reparation for sin, and petition.

The *Second Reading* comes from the Epistles (letters) that the apostles wrote to the first Christian Churches. Some of the advice was very practical, such as what to do with collection money or how to deal with troublemakers. But

for the most part the letters discuss how to grow in holiness, how to pray, and how to treat the people around us with true Christian charity.

Next we stand for the *Gospel*, to show our reverence for the words of Jesus. After we recite or sing the Alleluia verse, the priest

says: "The Lord be with you." The people answer: "And also with you." The priest goes on to say: "A reading from the holy Gospel according to Matthew" (or Mark, Luke, or John). Then the priest makes the Sign of the Cross on the Lectionary, and then on his forehead, lips, and heart. The people do the same as they answer: "Glory to you, Lord." The little crosses indicate that the word of our Lord is to be in our thoughts, on our lips, and in our hearts.

We hear the Gospel readings again and again, and we may be quite familiar with them. Why go over them so many times?

The Gospels are the record of what Jesus said and did on earth. Listening again and again to the teachings of Jesus or the stories about his miracles is a way to spend time with him, to know and love him better. The more we think about Jesus' life and words, the more we learn about him. We can never go over the gospels too many times; for every word and action is the word and action of God himself as he lived and walked among men.

So we must try not to drift off into daydreams during a familiar reading; God gives us special graces if we listen when he speaks to us.

In fact, we share the privilege of the disciples, to whom Jesus said: "Blest are the eyes that see what you see. I tell you, many prophets and kings wished to see what you see but did not see it, and to hear what you hear but did not hear it." (Lk 10:23–24)

Our Lord was talking about his own words and actions. He included in this privilege not only those who lived with him but all the people down through the ages who would do their best to get to know him by studying the accounts of his life, guided by the teaching and tradition of the Church.

Next comes the *Homily*, or *Sermon*. The readings and Psalm we have heard have been chosen to illustrate a theme. This theme may be developed by the priest in his Homily, and the meaning of Jesus' words and actions, which is sometimes hard to understand, is explained in light of the Church's teaching. The priest may talk about how we can apply what Jesus said and did to our own lives, and how understanding the Gospel can help us decide how to think and act.

At Sunday Mass, and on holy days or solemn (special) feasts, the Sermon is followed by the *Creed*, recited by everyone together. The Creed is a statement of what all Catholics believe. We have listened to Sacred Scripture, and the priest has explained it and applied it to practical cases; now it is time to express our faith in what God has revealed and taught us. In reciting the Creed we testify that we believe what God has revealed to men. We worship God, the author of all truth, with our minds.

The Creed is followed by the *General Intercessions* or *Prayers of the Faithful*. These prayers are for the needs of the Church, for our public authorities, for the salvation of the world, for those oppressed by any need, and for our local community and families.

This concludes the Liturgy of the Word.

"Man shall not live by bread alone, but by every word that proceeds from the mouth of God."

(Matthew 4:4)

"Speak Lord, thy servant is listening."

(1 Kings 3:10)

Liturgy of the Word

First Reading
Responsorial Psalm
Second Reading
Gospel
Homily (Sermon)
Profession of Faith (Creed)
Prayers of the Faithful

CHAPTER 24

Lift Up the Cup of Salvation

The **Liturgy of the Eucharist** begins with the *Preparation of the Gifts*. Bread, wine, and water are brought up to the priest from the people. The priest accepts them, places them on the altar, and with special prayers offers them to God.

All of the words and actions are rich with meaning. Whenever God wants to do something for us, he always does it in a way that helps our understanding; he uses a sign on one level that shows us what is happening on a higher level.

The bread and wine brought forward from the people will soon become the Body and Blood of Jesus. The bread is made up of many grains of wheat and the wine of many grapes, just as the people, though many, are made into the one Body of Christ through the mysteries of the Eucharist. We, though many, share the one bread and are made one.

The grapes were crushed in order to become wine, and the wheat was ground into flour to make bread. When we think of this, we can remember that we must die to ourselves, to our sins and faults, and live a new life in Christ.

At this time in the Mass we should be offering ourselves to God: our whole selves, including our joys and sorrows. A hymn may be sung that can help us understand the actions and the signs.

The *Prayers over the Gifts* acknowledge God's goodness as Lord of all creation and the goodness of creation itself. They ask God's blessing on these gifts which are to become for us the bread of life and our spiritual drink. After the priest offers the bread, and again after he offers the wine, the people respond, "Blessed be God forever."

The *Washing of the Hands* of the priest signifies the great purity with which we should approach the Eucharist. It is a prayer to God to wash away our sins as we come close to him.

The priest then invites the people to pray that our sacrifice may be accepted by God, the Almighty Father.

The people respond with a prayer that our sacrifice may be accepted at the hands of the priest for three purposes: 1. the praise and glory of God's name; 2. for our benefit; and

3. the good of all the Church. This prayer can remind us that in all that we do, God's glory must be considered first; our good and the good of all the Church, though very important, come second. With his hands extended, the priest then says a prayer that the gifts will be acceptable and pleasing to God. The people stand for this prayer and give consent to it by saying, "Amen".

The Eucharistic Prayer

Now comes the high point of the Mass, called the EUCHARISTIC PRAYER or CANON. It is in this part of the Mass that bread and wine become the Body and Blood of Our Lord and the sacrifice is offered to God.

The prayer begins with the *Preface*, a consideration of the coming sacrifice in light of the liturgical season of the year or of a feast day. It ends as we join our voices to those of the angels in Heaven in the hymn called the *Sanctus*:

"Holy, holy, holy Lord, God of power and might: Heaven and earth are full of your glory. Hosanna in the highest. Blessed is he who comes in the name of the Lord. Hosanna in the highest."

The word "hosanna" (a Hebrew word meaning "save us") is a special exclamation of joy in the salvation God has promised to us. It expresses our joyful expectation of God coming to us as our salvation.

The people, who were standing to give praise, now kneel and remain kneeling for the most solemn part of the Mass.

The priest extends his hands over the gifts and invokes the Holy Spirit, asking him to come upon them and make them holy so that they may become the Body and Blood of Our Lord Jesus Christ. Then he continues with the *Consecration*, in which he says: "This is my Body . . . this is the cup of my Blood."

The priest holds up the consecrated Host and then the chalice with the Precious Blood; as he holds them up for the people to adore, he and the people offer the Holy Sacrifice, Christ's Body and Blood, to our Heavenly Father.

This is the part of the Mass where we are called on to proclaim our belief in this great mystery of our faith—that Jesus really is present on the altar now.

The Canon also contains prayers for the Church, for the living, and for the dead. Then the priest takes the chalice and the paten with the Host and, lifting them up, says:

"Through him, with him, in him, in the unity of the Holy Spirit, all glory and honor is yours, Almighty Father, forever and ever."

This prayer is called a *Doxology*. The people respond with "Amen", which means that they fully assent to the prayer of the priest, and the sacrifice is complete.

Liturgy of the Eucharist

OFFERTORY

Preparation of the Altar
Preparation of the Gifts
Offering of the Gifts
Washing of the Hands
Prayers over the Gifts

EUCHARISTIC PRAYER
(CANON)

Preface
Sanctus
Prayer of Thanksgiving
Invocation of the Holy Spirit
Consecration
Offering to the Father
Doxology

"This first of all I ask, that petition, prayer, entreaty, and thanksgiving should be offered for all mankind."

(1 Timothy 2:1)

Q. 63 *When do the bread and wine become the Body and Blood of Jesus?*
The bread and wine become the Body and Blood of Jesus at the moment of the Consecration.

Q. 64 *After the Consecration is there anything left of the bread and wine?*
After the Consecration neither the bread nor the wine is present any longer, but there remain only the appearances of bread and wine.

CHAPTER 25

Come to the Table of the Lord

The COMMUNION RITE follows the Eucharistic Prayer in the Liturgy of the Eucharist. The sacred Victim, accepted by the Father—since it is his own divine Son—is now given back to us as the greatest gift we can receive.

At the conclusion of the Canon, after the people say "Amen", the priest puts down the chalice and the paten with the Host and says: "Let us pray with confidence to the Father in the words our Savior gave us."

Then we join in the *Our Father* in order to praise God and place our petitions before him. This is the prayer that Our Lord himself taught us as the model for all our prayers. It is certainly fitting, as we pause in the action of the

Mass, to reach out to God the Father with these words in which Jesus taught his apostles to pray simply, with confidence and love.

The Our Father, called the perfect prayer, contains all the spiritual ingredients we need to move us into a close and loving family, the People of God. Jesus taught us to say "our" Father, not "my" Father, because God wishes to live with us in a community. As God has said so many times in the Old Testament: "I will be your God and you will be my people."

My Peace I Give You

St. Paul, in his letter to the Philippians, speaks of the peace of God "which is beyond all understanding". (Phil 4:7) This priceless treasure of peace is Christ's gift to us. At the Last Supper, Christ says: "Peace is my farewell to you, my peace is my gift to you: I do not give it to you as the world gives peace. Do not be distressed or fearful." (Jn 14:27)

At this point in the Mass we may offer each other a sign of Christ's peace, the peace of forgiveness and the reassurance of having his mercy and love. To preserve this gift we must seek to live in peace every day with family and friends and everyone we meet.

As the *Rite of Peace* ends, the priest takes the Host and breaks it over the paten. He places a small piece in the chalice, saying quietly: "May this mingling of the Body and Blood of our Lord Jesus Christ bring eternal life to us who receive it."

Meanwhile, everyone prays: "Lamb of God, you take away the sins of the world, have mercy on us . . . grant us peace."

Jesus, of course, is the "Lamb of God"; he takes away the sins of the world. The Paschal lamb that is eaten by Jewish families to celebrate the Passover which freed the Israelites from the Egyptians is a symbol of the true Paschal Lamb who frees us from the slavery of our sins.

I Am Not Worthy

Close to Communion now, we repeat the words of a Roman Centurion who once asked Jesus to save one of his servants from death. The Centurion entreated Jesus not to bother coming to his house, since he did not consider himself worthy to receive Jesus, but simply to give the word and his servant would be cured. Jesus marveled at this man's faith and granted his request. Now we, too, say as the Centurion did:

"Lord, I am not worthy to receive you, but only say the word and I shall be healed."

Then the priest takes Communion, and the *Communion Antiphon* is recited or sung.

Finally we go up to receive Holy Communion. The priest holds the Host before the communicant, and says: "The Body of Christ", to which the communicant answers: "Amen". When we say "Amen" we are saying: "Yes, I believe that this is really Jesus Christ."

If we are unable to receive Communion for

some reason we should use the time to pray and ask Jesus to be present with us.

Giving Thanks

Receiving the Sacrament allows us to be alone with God in a private way. It is one of the best chances we have to thank Jesus for everything he gives us—especially the gift of his Body and Blood.

There is an incident in the Gospel in which Jesus cures ten lepers. They were cured as they were on their way to show themselves to the priests as Jesus directed. Only one of them returned to Jesus to thank him.

Let's remember to be grateful to Jesus for coming to us in Holy Communion. How do we welcome him? Do we receive him on our tongue or in our hand and then close our mind and heart to him? Do we at least keep him company for five or ten minutes?

When Communion has been distributed, the priest cleans the paten over the chalice and then cleans the chalice itself. The people have a chance to pray quietly. The priest may sit down for a time to continue the silence and thanksgiving. Then, standing at the chair or at the altar, the priest says the *Prayer after Communion*, which asks that our share in the Eucharist be fruitful.

The *Blessing* in the name of the Trinity follows, and then the priest declares: ''The Mass is ended, go in peace.''

The people answer: ''Thanks be to God.''

There may be a *Closing Hymn* (*Recessional*) as the priest leaves the altar.

After Mass, we should try to spend some time—however brief—alone with Jesus. We may pray for ourselves; for the Church, the pope, priests, and religious; for our families, friends, and others. A prayer book with a selection of prayers for thanksgiving after Communion may be a big help.

COMMUNION RITE

The Lord's Prayer (Our Father)
Rite of Peace
Breaking of the Bread
Lamb of God (Agnus Dei)
Communion of the Priest
Communion Antiphon
Communion of the People
Prayer after Communion

Blessing
Closing Hymn (Recessional)

Q. 65 *When the Host is broken into several parts, is the Body of Jesus Christ broken?*

When the Host is broken into several parts, the Body of Jesus Christ is not broken, but only the appearances of the bread; and the Body of Our Lord remains whole and entire in each of the parts.

Q. 66 *Is only the Body of Jesus Christ present under the appearances of bread and only his Blood under the appearances of the wine?*

No, under the appearances of the bread Jesus Christ is present whole and entire, in Body, Blood, Soul, and Divinity; and the same under the appearances of the wine.

CHAPTER 26

Preparing Our Hearts For Jesus

When we go up to receive Holy Communion, the priest holds the Host before us and says: ''The Body of Christ'', to which we respond: ''Amen''. We are expressing our belief in the Real Presence of Jesus before us under the appearance of bread and remembering that we have been called to unite ourselves with him in this most Holy Sacrament.

All of us are aware of our need for Jesus in our daily lives. Usually we feel this need most when we are suffering or struggling with a difficult problem. Jesus wants us to have confidence in him and not to worry:

> I tell you, do not be anxious about your life, what you shall eat, nor about your body, what you shall put on. For life is more than food and the body more than clothing. . . . Instead, seek his Kingdom; and these things shall be yours as well. (Lk 12:22−23, 31)

Receiving Jesus in Holy Communion should be a special occasion for us every time. Like all special occasions, we have to prepare for it. Before you take a big test you put in extra time studying. Or when a special friend comes to visit, you make sure everything is tidy or perhaps even make some sort of gift to give

that friend. We must also prepare to receive Jesus in Communion.

Jesus once told a parable about a king who gave a wedding banquet for his son. He invited everyone, rich and poor alike, until his hall was filled. When the king came in to meet his guests, he found one man who had not dressed properly for the wedding feast. When questioned, the man had nothing to say. The king's orders were: ''Bind him hand and foot and throw him out into the night to wail and grind his teeth.'' (Mt 22:13)

We will displease Jesus also if we go to Holy Communion without first being properly prepared.

We should always look to the example of Jesus to show us what is necessary. Remember how, at the Last Supper, Jesus washed the feet of his apostles? This was a sign that we are to receive him with purity and innocence of soul. We are all aware of our unworthiness to receive such a gift, but like the Roman Centurion we have confidence that Jesus will make us pleasing in his sight.

So how do we prepare our hearts to receive Jesus? It isn't something we do quickly just before we go to Mass. We should always be ready to meet Jesus. This means that we try to live according to Jesus' teaching. As followers of Jesus, our lives should be filled with prayer and good works. We should be unselfish and always ready to share with anyone in need. And most importantly, we must preserve that special life of grace in us which we first received in Baptism. If we lose that supernatural life through serious (mortal) sin, we should immediately ask God for forgiveness and renew his life in us by going to Confession.

The more we know about Jesus, the more we will love him and try to please him and want to be with him. We should receive him in Holy Communion often, with a sincere and humble heart, trusting in his great love and desire to be united with us.

Q. 67 *Is it a good and useful thing to receive Holy Communion frequently?*

It is a very good thing and most useful to receive Holy Communion frequently, even every day, provided it is done always with the right disposition.

Anima Christi

Soul of Christ, sanctify me.
Body of Christ, save me.
Blood of Christ, inebriate me.
Water from the side of Christ, wash me.
Passion of Christ, strengthen me.
O good Jesus, hear me.
Within thy wounds hide me.
Suffer me not to be separated from thee.
From the malicious enemy defend me.
In the hour of my death call me
And bid me come unto thee,
That with thy saints I may praise thee
For ever and ever. *Amen.*

CHAPTER 27

Come Lord Jesus

Jesus once asked his disciples, "Who do you say that I am?" Peter answered, "You are the Messiah, the Son of the living God." Jesus rejoiced at this answer because, he said, it was a revelation from God.

Jesus then declared that he would make Peter the Rock upon which he would build his Church. And he said, "I will entrust to you the keys of the Kingdom of Heaven. Whatever you declare bound on earth shall be bound in Heaven; whatever you declare loosed on earth shall be loosed in Heaven." (Mt 16:19)

One of the matters over which the Church has authority to bind and to loose is the administration of the sacraments. In other words, the Church has the power to make rules about these matters. The Church specifies the times and circumstances for the Eucharistic Sacrifice and for distribution of Holy Communion. She teaches us that there are three necessary conditions for the *worthy* reception of Holy Communion. We should:

1. be in the state of grace;
2. have a right intention;
3. observe the Eucharistic fast.

Let us look at these conditions.

State of Grace

The Church asks us, out of reverence for Christ, to be in the state of grace. This means that we may not go to Communion if we have committed a mortal sin and have not yet confessed it. To receive Communion in mortal sin would be another mortal sin, called *sacrilege*, the misuse of something holy. To receive Jesus without being in the state of grace would make us like that man in Jesus' parable who came to the wedding feast without being properly dressed.

Right Intention

To have the right intention, we must be aware of the meaning of the Eucharist: that it is Jesus himself whom we receive under the appearances of bread and wine. This means that we should receive him with humility and modesty, recognizing the fact that God is our Creator and we are his creatures.

How we behave at Mass, especially at Communion time, should reflect all these important attitudes. Looking around and talking to friends expresses disrespect and ignorance and gives a bad example.

We must intend to receive Jesus with faith, understanding, reverence, and a strong desire for the spiritual treasures which are to be had in the Blessed Sacrament.

Eucharistic Fast

The Eucharistic fast is a means of preparing to receive Jesus with ample time and consideration. It is a sign of our willingness to free ourselves from our own desires so that we can live as true followers of Christ.

We observe the fast by eating no food and drinking no liquids except water and medicine for one hour before receiving Communion. Those who are advanced in age or suffer from any infirmity, as well as those who take care of them, can receive the Holy Eucharist even if they have taken something during the previous hour.

Thanksgiving

Because the gift we receive in the Eucharist is so great, we should make a sincere thanksgiving afterwards. We may do so in set prayers or in our own words, expressing our own thoughts and hopes and fears, our troubles and our joys, our needs and our petitions.

Obligation

After all we have said about how wonderful this sacrament is, it may be a surprise that the Church has had to make a rule that requires all the faithful to receive the Eucharist at least once a year during the Easter season. The obligation is binding on all who have made their First Communion.

Viaticum

Communion given to one who is dying is called *Viaticum*, a Latin word meaning "provisions for a journey". It is well named. All through life Holy Communion has helped us get ready for a holy death. Viaticum is the final preparation for the journey from life on earth, through death, to life in Heaven.

So one departs for that Kingdom about which St. Paul said: "Eye has not seen nor ear heard, nor has it so much as entered man's mind, what things God has prepared for those who love him." (1 Cor 2:9)

We shall thank God then for every worthy and ardent Communion we have received.

Words to Know:

Eucharistic Fast
Viaticum   state of grace

Sweetest Jesus, may your most Sacred Body and Blood be the delight and sweetness of my soul, safety and firmness in every temptation, joy and peace in every tribulation, light and strength in every word and work, and final protection in death. *Amen*.

— St. Thomas Aquinas

Q. 68 *What is necessary for the worthy reception of Holy Communion?*

For a worthy reception of Holy Communion three things are necessary: first, to be in the state of grace; second, to recognize and to consider whom we are about to receive; third, to observe the Eucharistic fast.

Q. 69 *What does it mean to be in the state of grace?*

Being in the state of grace means to have one's conscience free of all mortal sin.

Q. 70 *What does it mean to recognize and consider whom we are about to receive?*

To recognize and to consider whom we are about to receive means that we should approach Our Lord Jesus Christ in the Eucharist with a living faith, with an ardent desire, and with deep humility and modesty.

Q. 71 *What does the Eucharistic fast require?*

The Eucharistic fast at present requires an abstinence of one hour from solid foods and all liquids except water.

Q. 72 *In danger of death, may one receive Holy Communion even without fasting?*

Yes, in danger of death one may receive Holy Communion without fasting.

Q. 73 *Is there an obligation to receive Holy Communion?*

Yes, we are obliged to receive Holy Communion every year during the Easter season, and also in danger of death as Holy Viaticum, which strengthens the soul for the journey into eternity.

CHAPTER 28

His Abiding Presence

We have seen that through transubstantiation Jesus changes bread and wine into his Body and Blood.

In this new reality, Jesus is contained in his entirety: Body, Blood, Soul, and Divinity. We have often referred to him as the God-man; and it is as the God-man that he comes to us in Holy Communion. We receive his Divinity as well as his humanity. We can truly say that God becomes our food.

Jesus promised his disciples that he would not leave them orphaned. Indeed, he has instituted a way to stay with us at all times. Jesus is present in the Blessed Sacrament which is kept in the tabernacles of our churches around the world. A lamp, called the sanctuary lamp, is kept burning there as long as the Blessed Sacrament is in the tabernacle.

Here, then, Jesus remains, night and day. He is truly Emmanuel—God with us. He dwells with us full of grace and truth.

We profess our faith in Jesus' presence in the Blessed Sacrament by our behavior in Church, including certain reverent actions: genuflecting, blessing ourselves with holy water, bowing our heads.

We are encouraged to visit the Blessed Sacrament when we have time and a church or chapel is open. The prayer we say there—our conversation with Jesus—is an extra act of love that we offer him freely, and it will win us special graces.

Eucharistic Worship

The Church has always encouraged devotion to the Blessed Sacrament. There are a number of forms of special Eucharistic worship outside of the Mass, which is, of course, the fountainhead of all the others.

One such form is a Eucharistic procession in which the Blessed Sacrament is carried through the streets with solemnity and reverence, accompanied by singing. Parishes often hold processions on the feast of *Corpus Christi*.

The most common form of Eucharistic worship outside the Mass, however, is Exposition and Benediction. The consecrated Host is put in a monstrance and placed on the altar for the faithful to see and adore.

During the Exposition there are prayers and hymns, and usually the Host is honored with incense. We express our profound adoration before the Real Presence of Christ.

At the end, the priest or deacon lifts the monstrance and blesses the faithful with it in the Sign of the Cross. This is called "Benediction".

Special Devotion

Throughout the ages there have been many saints who have had great devotion to Jesus in the Eucharist. St. Thomas Aquinas wrote many beautiful hymns for Eucharistic worship.

There is a saint of modern times, St. Peter Julian Eymard, who founded a religious congregation dedicated to the perpetual adoration of the Real Presence of Christ in the Blessed Sacrament. Priests of this order are called the Blessed Sacrament Fathers. The Blessed Sacrament is always exposed in their religious houses for perpetual adoration.

Words to Know:

Exposition	Benediction
monstrance	tabernacle

Act of Spiritual Communion

My Jesus, I believe that you are in the Blessed Sacrament. I love you above all things, and I long for you in my soul. Since I cannot now receive you sacramentally, come at least spiritually into my heart. I embrace you and unite myself entirely to you; never permit me to be separated from you.

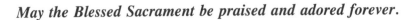

Q. 74 *Is Jesus Christ present in all the consecrated Hosts in the world?*
Yes, Jesus Christ is present in all the consecrated Hosts in the world.

Q. 75 *Why is the Most Holy Eucharist kept in the churches?*
The Most Holy Eucharist is kept in the churches so that the faithful may adore it, so that they may receive it in Communion, and so that they may recognize in the Holy Eucharist the perpetual assistance and presence of Jesus Christ in the Church.

May the Blessed Sacrament be praised and adored forever.

PART THREE

The Last Things

CHAPTER 29

Passage into Eternity

We are all children of Adam and Eve; we are all made up of body and soul, and condemned by original sin to the eventual parting of body and soul that we call death. This parting leaves the body without any life, and it falls back to dust. But the soul does not fall back into nothingness; the soul was made to live forever.

God gave us his very own Son to take the penalty of death upon himself to redeem us from sin. Through Jesus we have the hope of living in Heaven with God, although we must still undergo bodily death.

The bishops of the Catholic Church at the Second Vatican Council wrote: "Through Christ and in Christ the riddle of sorrow and death grow meaningful. . . . Apart from his gospel, they overwhelm us."

The mystery of death can only be answered by faith. With faith, we see death as it really is: a doorway, not a state.

Jesus said to his apostles, "Do not let your hearts be troubled. Have faith in God and faith in me. In my Father's house there are many dwelling places; otherwise, how could I have told you that I was going to prepare a place for you? I am indeed going to prepare a place for you, and then I shall come back to take you with me, so that where I am you also may be. You know the way that leads where I go." (Jn 14:1−4)

Every prayer we have ever said, every sacrament we have received, every good work we have ever done, every grace we have been given, helps to prepare us for the moment of death.

We ought to face death with hopeful joy, for Jesus said to Martha: "I am the Resurrection and the Life: whoever believes in me, though he should die, will come to life; and whoever is alive and believes in me will never die." (Jn 1:25−26)

Particular Judgment

Jesus, who knows our every thought, will judge each of us individually as soon as our souls leave our bodies. The truth of his verdict

will be made clear to us. With complete clarity we will immediately be aware of three things: 1. the exact balance of good and bad in our life and what we truly are; 2. the perfect justice of our future lot, in Heaven or Hell; 3. the presence of the Divine Judge, Jesus.

St. Paul says: "He will repay every man for what he has done: eternal life to those who strive for glory, honor, and immortality by patiently doing right; wrath and fury to those who selfishly disobey the truth and obey wickedness." (Rom 2:6−8)

Readiness

Jesus compares us to servants awaiting the return of the master of the house. He said, "Look around you! You do not know when the master of the house is coming." (Mk 13:35)

Jesus recommends a healthy awareness of the reality of death. It should not be a morbid thought; we just have to face facts. If we prepare ourselves for death, we will find joy and peace of mind that death cannot destroy.

We prepare for death by taking advantage of the means our loving Father in Heaven has given us. We do our best to live according to his will. We develop a spiritual life of prayer and the sacraments. We study the truths of our religion in school or at C.C.D., and afterwards we go on reading on our own and learn more about these truths.

Of course, we are aware that we often fail to keep God's laws, in little things if not in big; and so we must often turn to God's mercy and love. Knowing all this, the Church tells us how we can make up for our sins. We can offer prayers, especially the Rosary; we can do charitable deeds for others; we can do penance and offer sacrifices (for example, give up a dessert or second helping or give up having our own way about a television program).

Above all, we should serve God generously, not measuring everything with the minimum required by law. For Jesus said: "With your own measure it will be measured out to you again."

The closer we come to Jesus through prayer and acts of love, the more confidence we will have in his care for us and his mercy. If we live for him, we will learn more and more to see death as the beginning of a new and wonderful life with God.

Words to Know:

Particular Judgment

Q. 76 *What happens to each of us at the end of life?*
At the end of life each of us will die and face a Particular Judgment.

Q. 77 *On what will Jesus Christ judge us?*
Jesus Christ will judge us on the good and evil that we have done in life, including our thoughts and things we failed to do.

Q. 78 *After the Particular Judgment, what happens to the soul?*
After the Particular Judgment, if it is without sin and without a debt of punishment for sin, the soul goes into Heaven. If it has some venial sin or temporal punishment due for sin, it goes into Purgatory until it has made satisfaction. If it is in mortal sin, as a changeless rebel against God, it goes into Hell.

CHAPTER 30

Heaven – Purgatory – Hell

Heaven

We cannot know much about Heaven, only the little we have been told. Yet every time we look at a crucifix we are reminded that Christ was stripped of everything men hold dear and opened his arms on the Cross to gain for us our everlasting future of unimaginable happiness.

This does not mean that we should not try to think about true happiness, but only that we should always recall that the real thing will be far greater than anything we can think of. We can never make a mistake by exaggerating the happiness of Heaven. We can make a great mistake by thinking of it too little. An even greater mistake would be to make Heaven sound boring.

Living close to God prepares us for Heaven in many ways. Not only does it merit reward, but as the years go by we become more attuned to God and the things of Heaven, and that increases our desire to reach Heaven and our confidence that we will get there. "Taste and see that the Lord is good!" (Ps 34:8)

The purpose of your life and mine is to see God in Heaven someday. But that is not something that is easy to imagine: in fact, we cannot imagine God, since he is a pure spirit and we can only imagine things we have seen. So how can you get an idea of it? You can get an idea about it by thinking about the beauty and de-sign and order and truth and goodness and power of the world about you. Whatever God is, he is greater than all these. He is more beautiful, he is more powerful, he is more good, he is more true. Is the world exciting? It gets its excitement from him, just as it gets its goodness and beauty and power from him.

So now we can ask ourselves this question: What is Heaven? And we can say this: Heaven is being with God forever and loving God and living God's own life—which means seeing what God sees, doing what God does, knowing what God knows and loving and enjoying what God does to our fullest capacity. It means being like God!

We will not be bored; not for a moment.

Eternal life, therefore, means not only living forever, but living *God's life* forever!

God says: "My people will be filled with my good things."

Purgatory

It's easy to waste time out of thoughtlessness. We should use the minutes, hours, and days to grow in the spiritual life, to come close to God. Our spiritual life begins at Baptism, which removes the punishment for original sin but leaves us still with wounds in our nature.

Our life after Baptism, if it is a life of prayer, sacraments, and good works, will heal our wounds even more; if it is a life of sin and vice, it will deepen them.

There is a book about the spiritual life called *Ascent of Mount Carmel*, by St. John of the Cross. Growing spiritually is compared to climbing a great mountain. The higher we climb, the more we change. Some people climb all the way to the top and are rewarded with such union with God that they go straight to Heaven when they die.

Purgatory can also be compared to the ascent of Mount Carmel. Those who die as God's friends—in the state of grace, free of all sin or attachment to sin, free of all debt to make up for sin—go immediately to Heaven when they die. But what about those who die as God's friends, in the state of grace, but with unpaid debts for past sins, all forgiven but not yet worked off? They are not yet ready for Heaven. Only what is completely holy can enter Heaven. What happens to them?

They go to a place of purification and penance called Purgatory where their souls are cleansed and freed of the unpaid debt of sin.

Being purified hurts, both here and hereafter; there is no way to be healed and grow that is free from pain. But we can avoid a Purgatory in the hereafter by working off our Purgatory here. We can be healed and purified and make up for our sins by doing penance and by humbly accepting the difficulties and sufferings that come to us in life.

In Purgatory, there is one thing on everyone's mind: God. The soul there desires God with a greatness that is hard for us to imagine. The souls in Purgatory know with absolute certainty that they are saved and are going to Heaven. They fear no more danger to their salvation. They are being made ready for union with God, and so they must be cleansed of any obstacles to that perfect union. These obstacles to union are like rust, remains of sin that hinder the soul from enjoying God. St. Catherine of Genoa tells us that the rust diminishes as the soul becomes healthier under the rays of divine sunlight. So there is

great happiness as well as great suffering in Purgatory.

The saints in Heaven are called the Church Triumphant, the souls in Purgatory are called the Church Suffering, and the faithful on earth are called the Church Militant. All together we form the one Church of Christ. We on earth can help the souls in Purgatory by praying for them, sacrificing for them, and offering Masses for them.

Hell

Jesus told us that just as those who do the will of the Father will receive the reward of eternal happiness, those who reject the Father and refuse to do the will of God will be condemned to eternal punishment. "Out of my sight, you condemned, into that everlasting fire prepared for the devil and his angels." (Mt 25:4) The condemned are those who die without repenting of their mortal sins.

Many people like to think that Hell does not exist. They say that God would never send anyone to a place of everlasting torment since he loves us so much. It is true that God does not want people to go there. But he made us with a free will so that we could choose whether we would love God or only ourselves. Any persons in Hell have freely chosen to love only themselves; they are, of their own choosing, utterly alone.

The loss of God is the greatest pain in Hell. We were made for God, but since the souls in Hell have totally rejected him there is nothing left for them to hope for. And what makes their suffering in Hell even greater is that each one there will realize that he alone is the cause of his own damnation.

God offers everyone the grace to repent and turn to him. We should always remember to pray for those who are near death so that they will seek the mercy that God extends to them.

Words to Know:

Church Militant   Church Suffering

"What profit does a man show who gains the whole world and destroys himself in the process? What can a man offer in exchange for his life? If anyone in this faithless and corrupt age is ashamed of me and my doctrine, the Son of Man will be ashamed of him when he comes with the holy angels in his Father's glory."

(Mark 8:36—38)

Q. 79 *What does eternal life mean?*

Eternal life means that the reward, like the punishment, will last forever, and that the vision of God will be the true life and happiness of the soul, while being deprived of him will be the greatest unhappiness, like an eternal death.

Q. 80 *What is Purgatory?*

Purgatory is the *temporary* suffering of the lack of the vision of God and of other punishments, which remove from the soul the remains of sin, making it worthy of seeing God.

Q. 81 *Is it certain that Heaven and Hell exist?*

Yes it is certain that Heaven and Hell exist: God has revealed this, frequently promising eternal life and the enjoyment of himself to the good, and threatening the wicked with damnation and eternal fire.

Q. 82 *How long will Heaven and Hell last?*

Heaven and Hell will last forever.

CHAPTER 31

He Shall Come Again

St. Luke records in the Acts of the Apostles that at Jesus' Ascension into Heaven, two angels stood by the disciples and said to them, "Men of Galilee, why do you stand here looking up at the sky? This Jesus who has been taken from you will return just as you saw him go up into the heavens." (Acts 1:11)

One day, when we least expect it, Jesus will appear in the heavens in great splendor and majesty, and all the armies of Heaven with him. The trumpets will sound, the dead will rise, and the whole human race will be assembled before the judgment seat of Christ; the books will be opened and the Judgment will begin. Every man's deeds, even the most secret, will be made known. Everyone will see and appreciate the holiness of the just, whether they hardly ever sinned or were great sinners and overcame their sins. Everyone will see and appreciate the justice of God in banishing the unrepentant from his sight, into Hell forever.

The just, who served God with body and soul, in good times and bad, in good health and sickness, in joy and in sorrow, in pleasure and pain, will now receive a wonderful, glorious reward. They have tried hard to do something beautiful for God; now God will do something beautiful for them. It is true that they already see God, and this is called the Beatific Vision because it is a vision, a knowledge, which makes us "beatific" or *completely* happy. But as souls in Heaven they were not yet all that God made them to be. In full glory man was not made to be a disembodied spirit; man is a creature composed of body and soul. To be complete, body and soul must be brought together again. It is the whole man who will enjoy Heaven or suffer in Hell. There will no longer be any need for Purgatory.

One of the reasons for the Judgment at the end of the world, called the General Judgment, is to make clear to everyone the wisdom, knowledge, graciousness, mercy, patience, loving kindness, and justice of the Lord of History in his dealings with all men. All shall be satisfied that it was well done. Then the just, who so often suffered at the hands of the unjust, will be honored, and the unjust who refused to ask God's forgiveness will be covered with shame and disgrace.

Above all, Jesus Christ the Savior, who suffered such humiliations, will be fully vindicated, exalted, glorified, and honored. His splendor will be so great that he will light up the whole City of God. Perhaps the City of God, the new Jerusalem, the Heavenly City, will be the whole universe, once it is renewed and set free from anything unfitting or harmful. Then it will all be Heaven for those who have loved God and live in his light. And the just will have tremendous powers of mind and body to enjoy it all.

This is the goal toward which we are all striving. Remember how St. Paul compared the life of a Christian to an athlete's? Let us work toward our goal so that we can say with him:

I have fought the good fight, I have finished the race, I have kept the faith. From now on a merited crown awaits me; on that day the Lord, just Judge that he is, will award it to me—and not only to me, but to all who have looked for his appearing with eager longing. (2 Tim 4:7—8)

Words to Know:

Second Coming   General Judgment

Christ has died.
Christ has risen.
Christ will come again.

Q. 83 *Will Jesus Christ ever return to this earth in a visible manner?*
Jesus Christ will return visibly to this earth at the end of the world to judge the living and the dead, that is, all men, good and evil.

Q. 84 *What awaits us at the end of the world?*
The resurrection of the body and the General Judgment await us at the end of the world.

Q. 85 *What does "resurrection of the body" mean?*
The resurrection of the body means that our body will be refashioned and reunited to our soul, by the power of God, in order to participate during eternal life in the reward or punishment which the soul has merited.

Christmas Season Supplement

Angels We Have Heard on High

Legend has it that St. Francis of Assisi put together the first manger scene for Christmas with figures to inspire devotion—and that was about eight hundred years ago. The story of the birth of the Son of God has an endless appeal. For, considering who Jesus is, he chose for himself the humblest possible birth. He had every right to be born in a palace; he was born in a stable. He had every right to many servants; at most he had an ox and a donkey.

The Son of God did not come into the world

with power and glory. He did not come to establish an earthly kingdom. He came to redeem the human race from sin. His birth was the first step toward that end.

The Gospel tells us that the birth of Jesus came in "the fullness of time", that is, at the time God had chosen and prepared. He chose a virgin, Mary of Nazareth, to be the mother of his Son, and let her remain a virgin before and after his birth. Isaiah the prophet had written: "Therefore, the Lord himself will give you a sign: the virgin shall be with child, and bear a son, and shall name him Emmanuel." (Is 7:14)

Mary had been chosen by God from among all Jewish girls. He had chosen her to be the Mother of his Son and he preserved her from the stain of Original Sin. From the first moment of her existence she was free of this sin, which has been passed on to every other descendant of Adam. Mary's soul was created "full of grace", and she always cooperated with God's grace. She never sinned—not once, not even in the smallest way. She loved God so intensely that the fire of her love lit up all of history and was most pleasing to God. God made her first in importance among all the people who had a major role to play in his plan of Redemption—first after Jesus, that is. But she was not a princess. She lived with her parents in the small town of Nazareth and was engaged to marry a man named Joseph, a carpenter of the same town.

Mary was still a young girl, her marriage not far away, when God sent an angel to her on a very special mission. She must have been startled. The angel, Gabriel, told her not to be afraid. He told her that she had found favor with God and had been chosen to be the Mother of the Savior. He told her that she would conceive the Child by the power of the Holy Spirit; thus, she would always remain a virgin. Furthermore, the Child would be called ''Son of God''.

Mary's answer was: ''I am the handmaid of the Lord; let it be done to me according to your word.'' (Lk 1:38)

Then the angel left her, and God worked the miracle in which his only Son was conceived in her womb without an earthly father. When it became clear that Mary was going to bear a child, the same angel, Gabriel, told Joseph, Mary's fiancé, that Mary was with child by the Holy Spirit. This Child, he told Joseph, was to be named Jesus, because he would save his people from their sins.

So Joseph was relieved of a great anxiety, for he hadn't understood who the father of Mary's Child was. Now Joseph accepted Mary as his wife, and together they prepared for the Child's birth.

Not long before the Child was due, the Roman emperor decreed that there should be a census of the whole empire. Joseph had to take Mary with him to Bethlehem, the town of his ancestors, to register there for the census.

This involved a trip of about ninety miles, which must have been uncomfortable for Mary in her condition. Then, after the dusty, crowded roads, they found the houses and hotels in Bethlehem already filled. After asking every-

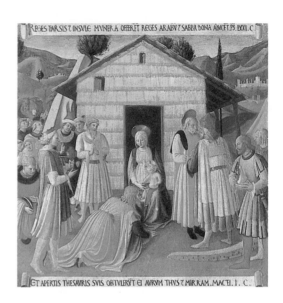

where, Joseph led his beloved wife to a stable, a cave in a hillside where she would be out of the cold night air and have privacy; and there, in that stable, the Son of God was born. There he gave his first cry and was laid down to sleep on some straw in a manger. He was wrapped in strips of cloth called swaddling clothes.

In the fields on some nearby hills, unusual things were happening. Angels came to some shepherds and told them to go to the stable to see the newborn Savior of the world. When the angels disappeared, the shepherds did what they had been told and found the Child. They were the first to see him. These shepherds weren't very powerful or important people, but they had what is always needed to find Jesus: humility. When they saw him, Luke tells us, they ''understood'' what they had been told about the Child.

Who is Jesus?

When Jesus cried, or felt chilled, or became hungry, it was God crying, or feeling chilled, or becoming hungry. He is the Son of God made man—that is, true God and true man. Before becoming man, he had eternal, infinite life with God the Father and God the Holy Spirit in the Blessed Trinity. This life was never interrupted, even when he became man; becoming man was something extra that he did.

Jesus is one Person, God the Son, with two natures, divine and human. As God, he can do everything God can do (know everything, create out of nothing, raise the dead, be everywhere, live eternally, love without limit), and as man he can do everything man can do—which is surely much less than what God can do.

The act by which the Son of God became man is called the Incarnation—which means, literally, taking on flesh. This happened when he was conceived in the womb of the Blessed Virgin Mary, and it was revealed for all the world to see when he was born.

That's how much God loved us—enough to become one of us.

Fruit Upon the Bough: The Mission

In his great mercy God gave to us his own Son to restore us to his friendship. Christ came into the world as an infant, bore witness to the will of the Father, taught us the complete truth about God, and was himself the perfect model of all we should be.

We call this Christ's mission. Even in Jesus' infancy, God began to reveal this mission to the world. We have seen how the shepherds were invited to come and see the newborn Savior. Not long afterwards, other things hap-

pened that showed that God was letting people know about Jesus' mission.

When Jesus was eight days old, St. Luke tells us he was circumcised in accordance with Jewish law; when he was forty days old, he was presented to the Lord in the Temple in Jerusalem. His parents offered in sacrifice two young pigeons, as the law directed.

Then a most unusual thing happened. A very devout old man named Simeon was led by the Holy Spirit to the Child in the Temple and took him into his arms. Through the Holy Spirit he recognized the Messiah. With great joy Simeon blessed God, saying that now he could die in peace because he had seen the Savior both of the Jews and Gentiles. Mary and Joseph marveled at what was being said.

Then the shadow of the Cross fell across the group—the Cross which was still far in the future. Simeon turned to Mary and said: "This Child is destined to be the downfall and the rise of many in Israel, a sign that will be opposed—and you yourself shall be pierced with a sword—so that the thoughts of many hearts may be laid bare."(Lk 2:34–35).

Simeon saw a full picture: power, glory, and suffering. The Child was a sign that would be opposed—and Mary, his Mother and Mother of the Church, would have a unique share in his sufferings. God was filling in the picture of his plan of Redemption.

Shortly afterwards, three kings or wise men from the East came to see the Child and give him gifts. God had told them to follow a bright star to find the newborn King of the Jews. Their visit was added testimony to the greatness of the newborn Savior; it was also testimony to the all-out fury which would oppose him.

King Herod, a vicious man insanely jealous of his power, heard from the wise men that a new King had been born, and all his darkest passions were aroused. Intending to kill the Child, he instructed the wise men to report back to him after they had found the Child. But the wise men were warned against Herod in a dream, and they went home by another route after their visit.

When Herod learned of this, his rage and suspicion knew no bounds. He sent his soldiers to Bethlehem and the surrounding area with orders to kill all the boys there who were two years old and younger, being certain that the newborn King would perish in the holocaust.

However, the Holy Family escaped the clutches of this bloodthirsty tyrant. Joseph had been warned in a dream of the coming danger. An angel commanded him to take mother and child and seek safety in Egypt and to stay there until he was told it was safe to come home.

Joseph obeyed immediately—that very night —and so they escaped. The children who died were Christ's first martyrs. We call them the Holy Innocents.

Not everybody is called to give his life for Christ—though many have. But it is sometimes as difficult to live for Christ as it is to die for him. It may even be harder. Take the case of a person with a serious illness who nevertheless has to bear heavy responsibilities. Think

of Pope John Paul II, who had to resume the burdensome task of the papacy after being so badly wounded. That must be harder than dying.

Another Stage

When Jesus was twelve years old, Luke tells us, he went to Jerusalem with his parents for the feast of the Passover. Unknown to them, he stayed behind when they set out on their return. At the end of the day they discovered he wasn't with them and returned immediately to Jerusalem to look for him. The third day they found him in the Temple, deeply involved in conversation with the teachers of the law, listening to them and asking them questions. Everyone who heard him was amazed at his wisdom.

Mary asked him why he had done this. He answered, ''Didn't you know that I must be about my Father's business?'' His parents did not understand. Afterwards he returned with them to Nazareth and lived in obedience, and Mary thought over all these things while he "progressed steadily in wisdom and age and grace before God and man". (Lk 2:52)

The unfolding of Christ's mission was often mysterious, even to his parents. In the Temple he had said, in effect, that he had reached adulthood, like turning eighteen or twenty-one in our society. According to Jewish law he was a man; and now that Jesus was an adult, the Father wanted his Son's witness in the Temple. He wanted his Son's wisdom to be known. But only this hint was given when Jesus was young; we hear no more until he is thirty years old and begins his public life. "Let your light shine before men", he was to say; and when he was twelve years old, he had begun to do so.

Until he entered upon his public life, Jesus lived quietly in poverty and humility, obedient in all things to the authority of his parents.

APPENDIX

ALB: a full-length white tunic worn by the priest when offering Mass.

AMICE: an oblong piece of white cloth worn by the priest under the alb covering his shoulders.

CHALICE: the cup-shaped vessel used at Mass to contain the Precious Blood of Christ.

CHASUBLE: the outer garment worn by the priest celebrating Mass.

CIBORIUM: a vessel with a lid used to hold the consecrated Hosts which we receive in Holy Communion.

CINCTURE: a cord tied around the waist of the alb.

COPE: a large semi-circular cloak worn by the priest at Benediction and in processions.

CORPORAL: a square white linen cloth on which the paten and chalice are placed during Mass.

CRUETS: small bottles or vessels that contain the water and wine used during Mass.

DALMATIC: the outer garment worn by a deacon at Mass or other liturgical celebrations.

FINGER TOWEL: a cloth used by the priest to dry his hands during the Mass.

HUMERAL VEIL: a long, oblong piece of cloth worn like a shawl over the priest's shoulders during Benediction when the priest holds the Monstrance.

LAVABO DISH or FINGER BOWL: a shallow dish for the water used when the priest washes his hands at Mass.

PALL: a stiff, square card covered with white linen used to cover the chalice at Mass.

PATEN: a plate of precious material on which the Body of Christ is placed during Mass.

PURIFICATOR: a small white linen towel used by the priest to purify the chalice and paten after Communion.

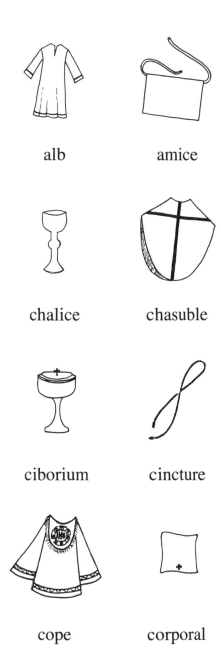

alb   amice

chalice   chasuble

ciborium   cincture

cope   corporal

STOLE: a long, narrow strip of cloth worn around the priest's neck during Mass; it is the same color as the chasuble.

VESTMENTS: special garments worn by the clergy at all liturgical celebrations. At Mass these include the amice, alb, cincture, stole, and chasuble. For Benediction the cope and humeral veil are used.

LITURGICAL COLORS

The different colors used throughout the liturgical year for vestments and decorations in the Church symbolize various truths and sentiments of the Faith.

WHITE: symbolizes purity, joy, innocence, holiness, and glory; it is used during the Christmas and Easter Seasons, for feasts and commemorations of Christ (other than the Passion) and for feasts and memorials of Mary, the angels, and saints who were not martyrs, and it may be used for Masses of the dead.

RED: symbolizes fire and blood; used for celebrations of the Passion, Palm Sunday, Good Friday, for Pentecost, for feasts of the Apostles and Evangelists, and for feasts of martyrs.

GREEN: symbolizes life and hope; used for days which are not feasts during Ordinary Time (the time after Epiphany up to Ash Wednesday and after Pentecost up to Advent).

VIOLET: symbolizes penitence and sorrow; used during the penitential seasons of Advent and Lent. It may also be used for Masses of the dead.

ROSE: is an indication of a more joyful celebration, and is used on Gaudete Sunday during Advent and Laetare Sunday during Lent.

BLACK: symbolizes mourning; it may be used in Masses for the dead, on All Soul's Day, and on Good Friday.

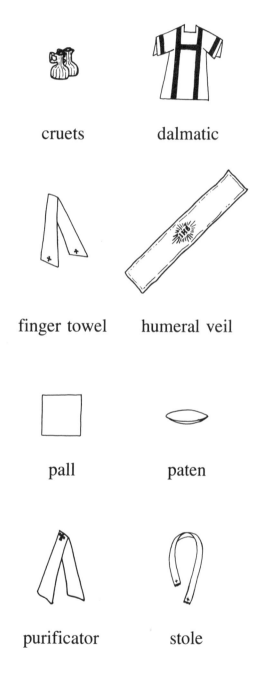

cruets   dalmatic

finger towel   humeral veil

pall   paten

purificator   stole

WORDS TO KNOW

ABSTINENCE: a form of penance such as refraining from eating meat.

ADORATION: giving praise and honor.

ADVENT: the liturgical season of four weeks before Christmas, during which we prepare for the birth of Jesus.

APOSTASY: the rejection by a baptized person of the Christian faith.

AVARICE: excessive desire for wealth; greed.

BEATITUDE: the promise of true happiness made by Jesus to those who follow him faithfully.

BENEDICTION: a Eucharistic devotion to Jesus in the Blessed Sacrament.

BLASPHEMY: the sin of speaking about or to God in a scornful or irreverent way.

CHASTITY: the virtue of ordering sexual pleasures according to the Sixth and Ninth Commandments.

CHURCH MILITANT: the members of the Church on earth.

CHURCH SUFFERING: the souls in Purgatory.

CHURCH TRIUMPHANT: the saints in Heaven.

CONSCIENCE: the capacity of our mind to know and judge what is right or wrong.

COVENANT: a solemn agreement.

CULPABLE IGNORANCE: not knowing something that one ought to know.

CURSING: the sin of expressing hope that evil or harm will happen to someone or something.

DECALOGUE: the Ten Commandments given to Moses by God.

DETRACTION: the sin of telling something without sufficient reason about another person that is true but harmful to that person's reputation.

DIVINE OFFICE: the prayer of the Church using psalms, hymns, and readings. It is called the Liturgy of the Hours because parts of it may be prayed at different times of the day.

ENVY: the sin of being resentful or saddened by another's success.

EUCHARIST: the real Body and Blood of Jesus under the appearances of bread and wine.

EUCHARISTIC FAST: abstinence from food and drink one hour before receiving Holy Communion. Water and medicine do not break the Eucharistic fast. The aged, the sick, and those who care for them may receive the Eucharist even if they have taken something during the previous hour.

EXPOSITION: the ceremony in which the Sacred Host is placed in a monstrance on or above the altar for adoration.

FALSE WITNESS: the giving of untrue testimony about another; lying about someone.

FASTING: doing penance by eating less food than usual.

FLATTERY: false praise.

FRAUD: the sin of deceiving another in order to deprive him of something he rightfully owns.

GENERAL JUDGMENT: the universal judgment of the entire human race at the end of the world.

GOSSIP: the sin of idle or malicious talk about others.

HERESY: the willful denial of a truth of faith.

HEROIC VIRTUE: the performance of extraordinarily virtuous actions.

HOLY DAYS OF OBLIGATION: certain days, besides Sundays, when Catholics are required to take part in Holy Mass.

HONOR: to respect and reverence someone or something.

IDOLATRY: the sin of worshipping something other than God.

IMPIETY: the sin of lacking reverence or proper respect for God.

IMPURITY: sexual pleasure in thought or action that is against the Sixth or Ninth Commandments.

INTERCESSOR: someone who pleads or prays for another.

LAST SUPPER: the last meal Jesus had with his apostles, at which he gave us the Eucharist, the Mass, and the priesthood.

LENT: the liturgical season of penance in preparation for Easter.

LITURGY: the public ceremonies of the Church used for worship.

LITURGY OF THE HOURS: see Divine Office.

MAKE SATISFACTION FOR: making up for some wrong-doing.

MEMORIAL: the recalling or remembrance of a past event.

MONSTRANCE: a special vessel used to hold and display the Sacred Host for adoration.

MURDER: the sin of killing someone wrongfully.

MYSTERY: a divinely revealed truth which we can never fully understand.

OATH: a declaration calling on God as a witness to the truth of what is being said.

OBLATION: the offering of something in an act of worship.

PARTICULAR JUDGMENT: the individual judgment by Christ of each human being at the moment after death.

PASSOVER: the Jewish feast commemorating the deliverance of the Israelites from Egypt.

PATRON SAINT: a special saint chosen to intercede for a particular person or group.

PENANCE: something done to make up for sin.

PRAYER: the raising of the mind and heart to God; talking with God.

PRECEPT: a particular rule or command.

RASH JUDGMENT: the sin of judging another's behavior as wrong without enough evidence.

REVERENCE: honor and respect.

SABBATH: the day of rest and worship; it is celebrated on Saturday by the Jews and on Sunday by Christians.

SACRAMENT: a sign given by Jesus that gives us grace.

SACRIFICE: the offering up of something to God.

SAINT: a holy person, particularly one who the Church has declared to be in Heaven.

SANCTITY: holiness.

SCANDAL: the sin of giving bad example which leads another into sin.

SECOND COMING: the return of Jesus at the end of the world as he promised at his Ascension.

SELF-DENIAL: the act of giving up something we desire for a higher motive.

SLANDER: the sin of saying something false about another which harms his good name.

STATE OF GRACE: being free of mortal sin and possessing God's grace.

STEALING: the sin of taking the property of another; this is a sin against the Seventh Commandment.

SUICIDE: the act of killing oneself; this is a sin against the Fifth Commandment. (However, if someone commits suicide without full knowledge and consent, his responsibility before God is lessened.)

SUPERSTITION: belief that creatures have supernatural powers.

TABERNACLE: a container in our churches in which the Blessed Sacrament is reserved.

TEN COMMANDMENTS: the laws given to us by God.

TRANSUBSTANTIATION: the complete change of substance of the bread and wine into the Body and Blood of Christ.

USURY: the sin of taking excessive interest for a loan of money.

VIATICUM: Holy Communion given to someone in danger of death.

VICAR OF CHRIST: the pope, who takes the place of Jesus on earth.

VICTIM: the thing offered to God in a sacrifice.

VOLUNTARY DOUBT: the sin of willfully doubting some religious truth when there is enough reason to believe it.

VOW: a solemn promise made to God of something good and pleasing to him.

WORSHIP: giving honor, praise, and sacrifice to God.

PRAYERS

THE SIGN OF THE CROSS

In the name of the Father, and of the Son, and of the Holy Spirit. *Amen.*

OUR FATHER

Our Father who art in Heaven, hallowed be thy Name. Thy Kingdom come, thy will be done on earth as it is in Heaven. Give us this day our daily bread, and forgive us our trespasses, as we forgive those who trespass against us, and lead us not into temptation, but deliver us from evil. *Amen.*

HAIL MARY

Hail Mary, full of grace, the Lord is with thee. Blessed art thou among women, and blessed is the fruit of thy womb, Jesus.

Holy Mary, Mother of God, pray for us sinners now and at the hour of our death. *Amen.*

GLORY BE

Glory be to the Father, and to the Son, and to the Holy Spirit. As it was in the beginning, is now, and ever shall be, world without end. *Amen.*

MORNING OFFERING

O Jesus, through the Immaculate Heart of Mary I offer thee my prayers, works, joys, and sufferings of this day in union with the Holy Sacrifice of the Mass throughout the world. I offer them for all the intentions of thy Sacred Heart: the salvation of souls, reparation for sin, the reunion of all Christians. I offer them for the intentions of our Bishops and of all Apostles of Prayer, and in particular for those recommended by our Holy Father this month.

THE APOSTLES' CREED

I believe in God, the Father Almighty, Creator of Heaven and earth; and in Jesus Christ, his only Son, Our Lord, who was conceived by the Holy Spirit, born of the Virgin Mary, suffered under Pontius Pilate, was crucified, died, and was buried. He descended into Hell; the third day he rose again from the dead. He ascended into Heaven, and is seated at the right hand of God, the Father almighty. From thence he shall come to judge the living and the dead.

I believe in the Holy Spirit, the Holy Catholic Church, the Communion of Saints, the forgiveness of sins, the resurrection of the body, and life everlasting. *Amen.*

ACT OF CONTRITION

O my God, I am heartily sorry for having offended thee. I detest all my sins because of thy just punishments, but most of all because they offend thee, my God, who art all good and deserving of all my love. I firmly resolve, with the help of thy grace, to confess my sins, to do penance, and to amend my life. *Amen.*

ACT OF FAITH

O my God, I firmly believe that thou art one God in three Divine Persons, Father, Son, and Holy Spirit; I believe that thy Divine Son became man and died for our sins, and that he will come to judge the living and the dead. I believe these and all the truths that the Holy Catholic Church teaches, because thou hast revealed them, who can neither deceive nor be deceived.

ACT OF HOPE

O my God, relying on thy infinite goodness and promises, I hope to obtain pardon of my sins, the help of thy grace, and life everlasting, through the merits of Jesus Christ, my Lord and Redeemer.

ACT OF LOVE

O my God, I love thee above all things, with my whole heart and soul, because thou art all good and worthy of all love. I love my neighbor as myself for the love of thee. I forgive all who have injured me and ask pardon of all whom I have injured.

MYSTERIES OF THE ROSARY

The Joyful Mysteries

1. The Annunciation.
2. The Visitation.
3. The Nativity.
4. The Presentation.
5. The Finding in the Temple.

The Sorrowful Mysteries

1. The Agony in the Garden.
2. The Scourging at the Pillar.
3. The Crowning with Thorns.
4. The Carrying of the Cross.
5. The Crucifixion.

The Glorious Mysteries

1. The Resurrection.
2. The Ascension.
3. The Descent of the Holy Spirit.
4. The Assumption.
5. The Coronation.

THE STATIONS OF THE CROSS

1. Jesus is condemned to death.
2. Jesus carries his Cross.
3. Jesus falls the first time.
4. Jesus meets his Mother.
5. Jesus is helped by Simon of Cyrene.
6. Veronica wipes the face of Jesus.
7. Jesus falls a second time.
8. Jesus speaks to the women.
9. Jesus falls a third time.
10. Jesus is stripped of his clothes.
11. Jesus is nailed to the Cross.
12. Jesus dies on the Cross.
13. Jesus is taken down from the Cross.
14. Jesus is placed in the tomb.

THE ANGELUS

V. *The angel of the Lord declared unto Mary.*
R. And she conceived of the Holy Spirit.
　　Hail Mary. . . .

V. *Behold the handmaid of the Lord.*
R. Be it done to me according to thy word.
　　Hail Mary. . . .

V. *And the Word was made flesh.*
R. And dwelt among us.
　　Hail Mary. . . .

V. *Pray for us, O holy Mother of God.*
R. That we may be made worthy of the promises of Christ.

Let us pray. Pour forth, we beseech thee, O Lord, thy grace into our hearts, that we, to whom the Incarnation of Christ thy Son was made known by the message of an angel, may by his Passion and Cross be brought to the glory of his Resurrection. Through the same Christ Our Lord. *Amen.*

MEMORARE

Remember, O most gracious Virgin Mary, that never was it known that anyone who fled to thy protection, implored thy help, or sought thy intercession, was left unaided. Inspired with this confidence, I fly unto thee, O Virgin of Virgins, my Mother: to thee do I come, before thee I stand, sinful and sorrowful. O Mother of the Word Incarnate, despise not my petitions, but in thy mercy hear and answer me. *Amen*.

PRAYER TO ST. MICHAEL

St. Michael, the Archangel, defend us in battle. Be our protection against the wickedness and snares of the devil. May God rebuke him, we humbly pray, and do thou, O prince of the Heavenly hosts, by the power of God, thrust into Hell Satan and the other evil spirits who prowl about the world seeking the ruin of souls. *Amen*.

ART CREDITS

METROPOLITAN MUSEUM OF ART, NEW YORK:

76   *Christ Crucified between Two Thieves*, 4th state, Rembrandt

PHOTOGRAPHS, GARY FUCHS:

pages 32, 34, 88, 89, 91, 94, 95, 96, 98, 99, 100, 110, 113

OTHER ART:

12   *Moses Presenting the Tablets*, Raphael, Vatican Polyglot
24   *St. Maximilian Kolbe*, Knights of the Immaculata
24   *St. Charles Lwanga*, The White Fathers of Africa
24   *St. John Bosco*, The Salesian Fathers
73   *The Last Supper*, Rosselli
78   *Supper at Emmaus*, 17th century tapestry, photo by Claveau